Inner Fitness
For Creating A Better You

Six Lessons for
Building Greater Awareness, High Self-Esteem,
Good Relationships, and Spiritual Meaning

Suzanne E. Harrill, M.Ed. – L.P.C.
Licensed Marriage and Family Therapist

Inner Fitness
For Creating A Better You

**Six Lessons for
Building Greater Awareness, High Self-Esteem,
Good Relationships, and Spiritual Meaning**

Copyright C 2003 by Suzanne E. Harrill
Updated 2007

All rights reserved. No part of this book may be reproduced or transmitted in any form or by any means, electronic or mechanical, including photocopying, recording, or by any information storage and retrieval system, without written permission from the copyright holder, except for handouts used for teaching purposes. Please give credit to the author.

Published by
Innerworks Publishing
167 Glengarry Place
Castle Rock, CO 80108 USA

www.InnerworksPublishing.com

ISBN: 1883648-11-4

ISBN: 1883648-12-2   e-book edition

I dedicate this book to:

Nancy Moonstarr, my sister
    and
Laura Mary Shaw, my mother

In appreciation, I thank Diane Langley for editing. Thank you Susan Pietrowski at Utopian Art (713-662-0561) for the beautiful cover design and my husband Rodney Harrill for the flower photograph.

Table of Contents
Inner Fitness for Creating A Better You

Two Ways to Use This Manual		iv
Lesson 1:	How Do You Feel About Yourself?	1
Lesson 2:	Building Self-Esteem Awareness	10
Lesson 3:	Things You Were Taught That Are *Not* True and Things You Were Not Taught That *Are* True	16
Lesson 4:	Who's the Matter with Me	26
Lesson 5:	Building Better Relationships	42
Lesson 6:	Spiritual Growth: Developing Deeper Meaning and Purpose in Your Life	57
Appendix I:	Self-Esteem Awareness Can Improve Your Effectiveness as a Group Facilitator	69
Appendix II:	Relationship Enrichment Cards	71

Free on-line newsletter, The Innerwords Messanger, to spark the inner journey.

www.InnerworksPublishing.com

Two Ways to Use This Manual

Let me start with a short background describing why and how *Inner Fitness for Creating a Better You* began. While living in Australia in the year 2000, a group of women, Vietnam veteran wives, in the city of Maitland, asked me to speak to them about self-esteem. One woman approached me afterwards and asked if I would train several of them to take the ideas presented to women in other chapters of their support network. This manual was originally created to train these women. Now I, and many others, use this course to facilitate awareness and self-discovery in others.

Inner Fitness for Creating a Better You can be used in two ways:

1. **Individually as a self-study course**. Here, you work at your own pace reading the manual, preferably out loud, and completing the assignments as you go. Journal writing is encouraged, as is taping the meditations with affirmations. A pack of 3x5 cards is needed for writing down affirmations.

2. **In a group setting with a facilitator**. Here the facilitator guides a class through six weeks of lessons. There are easy-to-understand directions at the beginning of each chapter explaining which handouts to copy for participants. Students are encouraged to buy a notebook for journal writing and 3x5 cards for writing affirmations. Some students prefer to own their own manual.

In the group setting, the course encourages participation and discussion through reading out loud. Each person, who so chooses, takes a turn reading paragraphs or points from the handouts. The reader may comment on what was just read or the facilitator may comment when someone in the group looks confused. It is not mandatory to read aloud. This method, of reading and then commenting, quickly builds group cohesiveness. After the fourth or fifth person, it becomes apparent that we all have things in common, especially on a feeling level. At this point people begin sharing and discussing the ideas more easily. The facilitator's job now is to help the group stay on task to complete the materials in the lesson. It is your call when to leave certain handouts out of the lesson in order to respond to time constraints, awareness level of the group, or the makeup of the group. For example, if a particular group is made up of mostly married people, there is no point in discussing in Lesson 5, **What You Should Know Before Saying, "I Do."**

With the group-reading-out-loud method of presentation, someone with little or no teaching experience can facilitate these six lessons. Seasoned teachers may choose more lecturing and less class reading. Professional speakers and therapists may use the materials to support their own presentations and psychotherapy.

It is helpful for the facilitator to read the whole manual to become familiar with the material before starting a group. It is designed to take six weeks for completion, meeting for 1 ½ or 2 hours, once a week. Short, simple directions begin each lesson, on pages 1, 10, 16, 26, 42, and 57. Feel free to change the length of time or the number of sessions that you meet, according to your needs and style of facilitating this course.

Now to be more specific, imagine you are ready to facilitate your first *Inner Fitness* course. Here are the steps for facilitating lesson one, **How Do You Feel About Yourself?**

Step One: Look at page 2, **Let's Get Started**. This session begins with a warm-up exercise, as do each of the others, to build feelings of safety and connectedness between group members. Begin by introducing yourself, then give each person a turn. Encourage each person to include why s/he is taking the class and what s/he hopes to gain. Even if some are uncomfortable expressing themselves, the anxiety level of the group lessens by hearing what others have to say.

Step Two: Read, or express in your own words, the introduction on page 2.

Step Three: Ask the group for their definitions of self-esteem, then read the definitions on page 3.

Step Four: Pass out the first handout, **Reflections on Myself**. (Throughout this manual I have indicated which pages to copy for distribution to the participants by simply placing the word "copy" in parentheses.) Read the directions to the group, emphasizing that this is a quick exercise and to jot down what easily comes to mind. Encourage people to read the paragraph that begins, I am a valuable... to themselves at bedtime and upon waking to set the tone for their day and begin focusing on improving how they feel. Changing negative thoughts, guiding beliefs, and self-talk impacts how one feels.

Step Five: Pass out **How Do You Feel About Yourself?** Read the first paragraph or summarize it in your own words. Suggest that during the next two handouts each participant check the points that strongly affect each of them. Now, ask each person who chooses to take a turn reading one of the bullets under **Signs of High Self-Esteem**. Emphasize that one may pass and not read aloud now or at any other time during the course. As each reads a point, suggest that s/he comments, gives an example, or simply says, "I agree with this statement." Allow room for disagreement. Your job as the facilitator is to keep it flowing. A comment from you helps to move things along; such as, "Thank you," or "Thank you for sharing," or "Good point." Make eye contact and nod your head to signal the next reader to take a turn.

Step Six: Proceed in the same way with **How Many People Have a Self-Esteem Problem and Do Not Even Know It**.

Step Seven: Read or summarize in your own words **Ways to Improve Your Self-Esteem**. Suggest each buy a notebook to use for journal writing and a pack of 3x5 cards on which to write affirmations during the course.

Step Eight: The last handout, **Take a Look at Your Needs**, may be given as homework. Read the first two paragraphs out loud and encourage students to list their needs. It is okay to use some already listed as examples.

Step Nine: About 5 - 10 minutes before the end of the session begin the closing. Ask questions such as, what impacted you the most from this lesson or what are you willing to do this week to build your self-esteem? You might suggest that people exchange phone numbers after class to encourage building a support system that continues beyond the course. Some group members bond and begin meeting for coffee or dinner after a couple of lessons.

Self-esteem is an important foundation of this course. Included in the appendix is **Self-Esteem Awareness Can Improve Your Effectiveness as a Group Facilitator**. It is helpful to remember that you are learning and growing too. You can only do your best and there will be times when a group clicks and you do an exceptional job facilitating and other times when it just does not meet your standards. This is part of the learning process in working with others and yourself. As you become more familiar with the ideas presented here, you will gain confidence in teaching in your own, unique way and you will develop the skills to adapt the materials to fit each particular group.

I continue to learn from these ideas and I have been teaching and facilitating others for over twenty-five years. I remind myself often that I am a student too and that I am teaching what I am learning. I always learn from the people in the classes.

As more individuals learn about these ideas and apply them, the world becomes a better place. The world heals as individuals heal themselves. I send you good thoughts as you use this manual for self-study or to pass on the ideas in *Inner Fitness for Creating A Better You* to others. Thank you for the part you play in healing yourself and others.

Love and Blessings,

Suzanne

Lesson 1: How Do You Feel About Yourself?

I. **Let's Get Started.** After the introductions you may read **Let's Get Started** or express it in your own words.

II. **Define Self-Esteem.** (Copy) Ask for definitions, read the definitions on the handout and discuss.

III. **Reflections on Myself.** (Copy) Read the first two paragraphs to the group and then ask them to write their answers to the three questions. When most are finished, ask who feels comfortable sharing her/his answers. Discussion follows. Encourage people to read this healing paragraph of affirmations to themselves every day upon awakening and retiring at night.

IV. **How Do You Feel About Yourself?** (Copy) Read or summarize the first paragraph. Take turns reading **Signs of High Self-Esteem**. Encourage comments as you go. Ask each person to check in the margin the ones that are important personal issues needing attention.

V. **How Do Many People Have a Self-Esteem Problem and Not Even Know It?** (Copy) Read the first four bullets. The group takes turns reading **Signs of Low Self-Esteem** and commenting, checking in the margin relevant issues. Group discussion. Ask for questions and clarify issues.

VI. **Ways to Improve Your Self-Esteem.** (Copy) Read and discuss. Take a moment to reflect, then write on the back of the page, what you are willing to do during this course to build self-esteem. (Copy **Journal Questions**.)

VII. **Take a Look at Your Needs**. (Copy) Read top paragraph and allow class time to list their needs. Discuss.

VIII. **Closing.** Group sharing. What impacted you the most today? What will you put into practice this week to build your self-esteem? What is difficult for you? Allow additional comments. Encourage the exchange of phone numbers and suggest that over time some might like to meet for coffee or dinner before or after the class.

Let's Get Started
Creating a Better You

Warm up: Everyone introduces her/himself, including the facilitator, and shares what each hopes to gain from this course. This takes 5 - 10 minutes.

Introduction: This class is about becoming your own best friend, strengthening the foundation of your life with healthy self-esteem and better relationships. You empower yourself by taking charge of the one thing you have control over in life, your inner self. Your beliefs and attitudes color all that happens to you. Why not play the hand you were dealt with more awareness? It begins with a decision to get to know yourself better and to take care of yourself on all levels: physical, emotional, mental, and spiritual. A well-nourished self is creative, energetic, joyful, giving, has rich and meaningful relationships, and is continually growing. This is the path on which this course will lead you.

We will spend a lot of time gathering information and implementing ideas to build a stronger foundation of healthy self-esteem in your life. To some of you this may be your first experience in a self-discovery course and getting to know yourself at a deeper level. To others it will be a reminder of what you already know and will give you the opportunity to put into practice those things you know are good for you. Awareness levels will vary and it is very important to stop comparing yourself to others. You are encouraged to go at your own pace and participate at the level in which you are comfortable.

Our weekly lesson will stimulate many thoughts and feelings. Journal writing is an important key to getting more out of this course. If you do not journal write already, get a notebook and try it for the duration of this class. Even if you initially resist, stay with it for six weeks to test out whether or not it is a helpful tool for you. We will discuss journal writing in more detail a little later. Also, buy a pack of 3x5 cards on which to write affirmations that speak to you during the course. Read them to yourself often.

One more thing before we start our class — confidentiality. We respect each other's privacy and do not discuss the names of group members or personal details of the things members choose to share that would identify them to others outside of the group.

Definitions of Self-Esteem

"Self-Esteem, on a subtle and often unconscious level, is an emotion, how warm and loving you actually feel toward yourself, based on your individual sense of personal worth and importance. It is how you feel about yourself."
    L.S. Barksdale, *Building Self-Esteem*

"The measure of how much we like and approve of our self-concept."
    Linda Tschirhart Sanford & Mary Ellen Donovan, *Women & Self-Esteem*

"Self-Esteem is the experience of being capable of managing life's challenges and being worthy of happiness."
    National Association for Self-Esteem

"Appreciating my own worth and importance and having the character to be accountable for myself and to act responsibly toward others."
    California Task Force, *Toward A State of Esteem*

"Self-esteem is how you feel about yourself, based upon your personal evaluation of yourself. You consciously and unconsciously send thoughts, opinions, and images of yourself *to* yourself. Your perceptions, beliefs, and self-concept may or may not be accurate.
    Suzanne E. Harrill, *Enlightening Cinderella Beyond the Prince Charming Fantasy*

Add some of your own.

Reflections on Myself

Read the following paragraph and notice the degree of truth for you. You may feel the statements are true, somewhat true, or false. If they are not true for you, begin the healing process by saying these affirmations often to yourself. This will repattern your inner belief structure over time to give you a different experience of life.

I am a valuable, worthwhile person. I deserve love, respect, good relationships, health, and work that uses my abilities. I am capable of living peacefully with others, able to communicate well, to problem-solve, and to resolve conflict. I forgive myself for not being perfect and learn from my mistakes. As I take positive risks to change within, I notice my outer world changes. I enjoy my life, feel good, and I love the person that I am.

1. What parts of the paragraph make you uncomfortable? are not true for you?

2. What gets in the way of this being true for you?

3. Where in your life do you notice feelings of low self-esteem? high self-esteem?

Suzanne E. Harrill, M.Ed., Counselor, Teacher, Author: www.InnerworksPublishing.com

How Do You Feel About Yourself?

Happiness, self-empowerment, satisfaction in work, good relationships, and success are all built on a foundation of healthy self-esteem. **High self-esteem** is a quiet, comfortable feeling of acceptance and love for yourself – as you are. It is respecting and valuing yourself as a worthwhile human being, honestly seeing your good and not-so-good qualities, and taking care of and nurturing yourself so you can become all that you are capable of being. High self-esteem is characterized by congruence between inner states (beliefs, feelings, attitudes) and outer states (behaviors, relationships, health). A person with high self-esteem is self-aware, takes responsibility for life choices by being willing to pay consequences both good and bad, and is actualizing her/his potential. S/he also lives from a place of deep peace with the intention of honoring and respecting self and all others.

Signs of High Self-Esteem

- Having an internal locus of control, getting *okayness* from within, not from others.
- Taking care of yourself – physically, emotionally, mentally, and spiritually.
- Maintaining a balance between extremes of thought, feeling, and behavior. When out-of-balance, taking action to correct.
- Learning from mistakes and being able to say, "I made a mistake." If it involves another person, being able to make amends or say, "I'm sorry." Able to forgive self and others.
- Managing your life responsibly.
- Honoring individual differences among people.
- Listening to other points of view.
- Taking responsibility for your own perceptions and reactions; not projecting onto others.
- Having the ability to listen to your wise inner self (your intuition), and to act on this guidance.
- Knowing your own strengths and weaknesses.
- Choosing continuous self-improvement and taking positive risks.
- Balancing being and doing.
- Feeling warm and loving towards self.
- Giving and receiving love easily, with no strings attached.
- Demonstrating self-respect, self-confidence, and self-acceptance.

Suzanne E. Harrill, M.Ed., Counselor, Teacher, Author: www.InnerworksPublishing.com

How Many People Have A Self-Esteem Problem and Do Not Even Know It

- Some people with low self-esteem are overachievers who believe that a high IQ, physical beauty, winning at sports, or being *Number One* assures emotional well-being. They are often motivated by feelings of inferiority that propel them to seek validation of worth (their own and other's) in outer manifestations; such as, money, power, or praise.

- Some people make a practice of devoting all of their time and energy to family and friends and none to themselves. Often they give for the wrong reasons, with hidden agendas and expectations; such as, to be loved, admired, or needed. Unfulfilled people are secretly needy and give conditionally.

- Some believe that they can only be loved by earning love and *doing* something. They then evaluate their worthiness based on what they do, not on who they are.

- Some base their self-worth on the opinions of others or on outside indicators, such as the value of their portfolio in the stock market. Turning power outside of self, these people feel like victims.

Signs of Low Self-Esteem

- Self-blame, self-criticism, or constantly putting others down through guilt, blame, shame, or faultfinding. Finding forgiveness difficult.
- Over- or under-achieving, -eating, -working, -doing, etc.
- Playing the victim, rationalizing that outside circumstances are the causes of your problems.
- Not taking responsibility for your own life; turning power over to another to make decisions for you, then feeling victimized if the results are not to your liking.
- Taking too much responsibility for the lives of others, dominating and making decisions for them.
- Fear of change and reluctance to take risks. Or too much change, taking dangerous, unwise risks.
- Constant negativity or being so optimistic that reality is denied.
- Reacting to others with extreme emotion or no emotion.
- Boastfulness, lying, embellishing, exaggerating, and overbearing behavior around others.
- Inability to maintain integrity during interactions with others.
- Demanding to be "right," needing to have agreement or have your own way most of the time, or constantly acquiescing to the will and opinions of others.
- Constantly comparing yourself to others, thereby feeling inferior or superior.
- Black/white, either/or thinking; e.g., believing that a person is either good or bad based on rigid standards of behavior.
- Having pervasive deep-seated feelings of fear, terror, or panic.
- Speaking with lots of *shoulds, oughts, could haves,* and *yes, buts*.
- Interpreting the hurtful words or actions of others as proof of your unworthiness.

Suzanne E. Harrill, M.Ed., Counselor, Teacher, Author: www.InnerworksPublishing.com

Ways to Improve Your Self-Esteem

1. Change your negative self-talk. Everyone has a voice inside her/his mind that is continually commenting. The negative, critical, hurtful comments need to be changed. Begin listening to what you say to yourself and then talk back to your negative self-talk with the truth. Speed up the process by saying positive statements or **affirmations**; such as, "I like myself and am a worthwhile person, I forgive myself for not knowing/being/doing…, I deserve love, inner peace, and fulfillment." Make a cassette tape, in your voice, of affirmations. Listen daily.

2. Visualize what you want to create in your life. Picture what you want to create, whether it is a new dress or feeling confident in new situations. When you combine an affirmation, with deep feeling, and with a positive mental picture you add power to what you want to create. Look for pictures in magazines that picture what you want to create and glue them into your journal.

3. Nurture yourself. Take care of yourself physically, emotionally, mentally, and spiritually. Enjoy the times when others are able to nurture you or meet your needs; watch the tendency to set yourself up for disappointment with unreal expectations.

4. Build a support system. You deserve to have at least one person to talk to who accepts you without judging you. Consider joining a group to meet new people.

5. Take time to be alone daily. Spending quality time alone allows you to listen to your inner self. It is time to think, read, write, pray, meditate, or listen to your intuition.

6. Use your talents. Develop your interests. Take classes, find a teacher to begin.

7. Keep a journal. Writing is a good way to get to know yourself, solve your problems, lower your stress level, and balance yourself emotionally. If you have never written before, begin by writing for 20 minutes a day for the duration of this course. Include your thoughts, feelings, and emotional reactions to people and situations that have upset or hurt you. Eventually, insights and wisdom, that under normal circumstances are hidden from you, flow onto the paper. Do not worry about spelling or grammar. Consider using different colored inks to write according to how you feel. Writing clarifies your thoughts, feelings, needs, wants, visions, values, goals, and priorities and helps you communicate better with others. Following are questions to get you started.

Suzanne E. Harrill, M.Ed., Counselor, Teacher, Author: www.InnerworksPublishing.com

Journal Questions to Get You Started

1. Write about the people and situations that influenced your self-esteem, both positively and negatively, in your early life, as an adolescent, and as an adult? What would you like to say to them or about them right now?

2. Write about the things you are grateful for in your life? Update this often.

3. List your needs. Think about needs in five different areas: physical (healthy food, regular exercise), emotional (affection, one person to share intimately with that does not judge you), social (belong to a group, people to play with), mental (stimulating ideas to keep you growing, explore an interest), and spiritual (quiet time to be alone—being instead of doing).

4. Write about significant emotional events that have affected you positively and negatively.

5. What does forgiveness mean to you? Where might you practice forgiveness?

6. Discuss three short-range goals you have for yourself? List the steps you see as necessary to achieve them. How will these goals affect others in your life?

7. What gives your life meaning? List your values (quality time with family, being debt-free and saving money, integrity, kindness) What do you like about your life? want to change?

8. Write about a close friend and/or mentor in your life. Describe their impact on your life. Is it easy or difficult to accept help from another? Write about this. How might you go about finding a friend or mentor if you do not have this in your life?

9. Discuss your experience with conditional and unconditional love.

10. Write about your wishes, hopes, and dreams.

11. Record your nighttime dreams. Write about your feelings, insights, and messages.

12. List things you are proud of and things you like about yourself.

13. Discuss your greatest fear and its effect? What do you want to do about it?

14. Write letters to people with whom you are angry, feel have hurt or neglected you, or anyone you feel you treated unjustly. These letters are not to send.

15. What are the major themes in your life? What lessons do you feel you have learned thus far within these themes? What do you still have to learn?

16. What did you learn about expressing your creativity from your mother? your father?

17. Write your autobiography, then how your past can positively impact your future.

Take a Look at Your Needs

Psychologist Abraham Maslow explained that people are motivated to satisfy their basic needs. Using a pyramid with five levels, he said that as the lower levels of needs are satisfied, people move up the Hierarchy of Needs ladder.

The bottom level describes physical needs as the most basic needs to survive and stay alive — food, air, water, sleep, protection from heat and cold, pain avoidance. At Level 2 security needs for safety and protection are important. Level 3 is meeting social needs to respond and communicate; love, belonging, and closeness are important. Level 4 is where self-esteem needs are met to respect one's self and receive respect from others. Level 5 is the need for self-actualization or to realize one's potential; creativity, imagination, and self-motivation are important here.

Where do you see yourself operating with Maslow's Hierarchy of Needs? Why?

Use Maslow's categories to assess your current needs and help you figure out ways to improve your life. Here are some examples of needs you may have:

Physical needs: to eat healthy food, to get enough sleep, to exercise

Security needs: move to a safer neighborhood, leave an abusive job or relationship

Social needs: join a group to build feelings of belonging, make a new friend that accepts you as you are, take risks to smile more to show kindness to others

Self-Esteem needs: quality time alone to ponder, meditate, read, etc. in order to do the inner work necessary to become your own best friend, say affirmations to change your negative self-talk, always tell yourself the truth about what you are feeling

Self-Actualization needs: to become more aware, to express interests and talents, to heal and grow, to create, to daydream or visualize possible futures, to meditate on your spiritual purpose, to actualize ideas, to be proactive with solutions to problems

List some of your needs. Check the ones that you know or feel must be addressed at this time. _____
_____
_____
_____
_____
_____
_____

Suzanne E. Harrill, M.Ed., Counselor, Teacher, Author: www.InnerworksPublishing.com

Lesson 2: Building Self-Esteem Awareness

I. **Warm up:** Ask each person to share something they did to build their own self-esteem in the past week. If someone reports no progress or action, emphasize that it is okay, as each is at a different place on her/his life journey. Some are gathering information while others are ready to change.

II. **Harrill Self-Esteem Inventory.** (Copy) Read the directions out loud, explaining this is not a test and does not measure one's self-esteem level. It simply shows areas that block feelings of self-worth and need to be addressed. After everyone is finished, discuss. Some groups like to go over each point, while others like to discuss the low-scoring ones. Encourage people to retake this again at the end of the course and once a year.

III. **Affirmations** are positive statements to override negative self-talk and outdated beliefs. Each statement in the self-esteem inventory is an affirmation to heal beliefs that perpetuate low self-esteem. Pass out 3x5 cards to write down low-scoring statements from the inventory. Tape them around the house as constant reminders of new beliefs. Suggest reading them daily, preferably when awakening and before falling asleep at night.

IV. **Things Your Family May Never Have Taught You About Self-Esteem.** (Copy) Take turns reading and commenting upon each statement.

V. **Acorn Analogy.** (Copy) Read. Answer the questions with a partner and then discuss in the larger group. If you have acorns (wooden, clay, paper, or real ones), pass them out as a symbol for the potential hidden inside each of us. Read and Discuss Self-Care Tips.

VI. **60 Ways to Nurture Yourself.** (Copy) Ask the group to read silently and add some of their own to the list. Discuss ways we nurture self and ways we neglect self-care. Why do we forget to take care of ourselves? Suggest everyone set self-care as a priority and agree to practice at least one new way to nurture her/himself this week. Write it down as a reminder.

VII. **Closing: I Am My Self.** (Copy) Read out loud or as a guided meditation, suggesting each close their eyes, deep breathe, and imagine themselves in a peaceful place. Suggest that one's future self is speaking to them and the statements are already true. When finished, ask each to bring the awareness back to the room, feeling rested, and able to drive home safely.

The Harrill Self-Esteem Inventory

Rate yourself on each with a scale of 0 to 4 based upon your current thoughts, feelings, and behaviors:
0 = I never think, feel, or behave this way. **1** = I do less than half the time. **2** = I do 50% of the time.
3 = I do more than half the time. **4** = I always think, feel, or behave this way.

Score	SELF-ESTEEM STATEMENTS

_____1. I like and accept myself right now, even as I grow and evolve.

_____2. I am worthy simply for who I am, not what I do. I do not have to earn my worthiness.

_____3. I get my needs met before meeting the wants of others. I balance my needs with those of my partner and family.

_____4. I easily release negative feelings when other people blame or criticize me.

_____5. I always tell myself the truth about what I am feeling.

_____6. I am incomparable and stop comparing myself with other people.

_____7. I feel of equal value to other people, regardless of my performance, looks, IQ, achievements, or possessions (or lack of them).

_____8. I take responsibility for my feelings, emotions, thoughts, and actions. I do not give others credit or blame for how I feel, think, or what I do.

_____9. I learn and grow from my mistakes rather than deny them or use them to confirm my unworthiness.

_____10. I nurture myself with kind, supportive self-talk.

_____11. I love, respect, and honor myself.

_____12. I accept other people as they are, even when they do not meet my expectations, or their behaviors and beliefs are not to my liking.

_____13. I am not responsible for anyone else's actions, needs, thoughts, moods, or feelings, only for my own (exception, my own young children).

_____14. I feel my own feelings and think my own thoughts, even when those around me think or feel differently.

_____15. I am kind to myself and do not use "shoulds" and "oughts" to put myself down with value judgments.

_____16. I allow others to have their own interpretation and experience of me and realize I cannot control their perceptions and opinions of me.

_____17. I face my fears and insecurities, taking appropriate steps to heal and grow.

_____18. I forgive myself and others for making mistakes and being unaware.

_____19. I accept responsibility for my perceptions of others and for my response to them.

_____20. I do not dominate others or allow others to dominate me.

_____21. I am my own authority. I make decisions with the intention of furthering my own and others' best interests.

_____22. I find meaning and have purpose in my life.

_____23. I balance giving and receiving in my life. I have good boundaries with others.

_____24. I am responsible for changing what I do not like in my life.

_____25. I choose to love and respect all human beings regardless of their beliefs and actions. I can love others without having an active relationship with them.

This is not a test or a precise measure of self-esteem. It identifies beliefs, feelings, and behaviors that affect low self-esteem.

Suzanne E. Harrill, M.Ed., Counselor, Teacher, Author: www.InnerworksPublishing.com

Things Your Family May Never Have Taught You About Self-Esteem

1. A high IQ, physical strength, beauty, or achievements do not insure emotional health.

2. It is healthy to love and nurture yourself before saying "yes" to others' wishes or needs. It is important to balance giving and receiving.

3. It is important to identify and to get your needs met before fulfilling your wants.

4. Set emotional boundaries that support you. You have the right to say "no."

5. You are worthy of love and respect; it is not based upon what you do, but who you are.

6. You are of equal value to all other people, no more or less worthy. Stop comparing yourself.

7. If you act bad or make a mistake, you are not a bad person. Separate *You* from your behavior.

8. To feel better about yourself or change unwanted behavior patterns, look at your conscious and unconscious needs and the guiding beliefs motivating you.

9. Stop blaming, criticizing, or value judging yourself and others. Watch your *shoulds* and *oughts*.

10. Be honest with yourself so you can make choices that support you, using your heart and head.

11. You, and only you, are responsible for your life and can work through and forgive past hurts.

12. Say positive, supportive, encouraging things to yourself with your self-talk. Correct limiting beliefs.

13. Your attitude determines how well you manage your challenges and are able to enjoy your life.

14. Self-awareness is important to help you change and grow. Admitting what you do not like in yourself opens the door for healing. You are capable of learning new things to help yourself.

15. It empowers you to know your inner self. Your true self can direct your life, enabling you to overcome your conditioning and help you to live from a place of integrity, balance, and strength.

16. Make amends when you have hurt another. As you grow in loving and forgiving yourself, you cannot intentionally hurt another.

17. Know and accept your strengths and talents. Use them to grow into your full-potential Self, living a life with meaning and purpose.

18. When you love yourself, you are a mirror to help others love themselves.

Suzanne E. Harrill, M.Ed., Counselor, Teacher, Author: www.InnerworksPublishing.com

The Acorn Analogy

Deep inside you know how to be you,
    as an acorn knows how to be a mighty oak.

The acorn does the best it can do
    at each stage of growth along its life path.

Even if the early start was less than perfect
    the eager oak accelerates its desire to grow
    every time that it has nurturing from nature:
    sunlight, rainwater, and soil nutrients.

YOU are like the acorn doing your best
    under the conditions in which you are growing.

Nurture yourself with awareness, acceptance, love,
    self-respect, and self-esteem, then watch
    you grow towards your full-potential Self!

Self-Awareness Questions:

1. What nutrients do you need to help you grow? Check the ones you can provide yourself.
2. How does this analogy help you forgive unaware choices you have made in your life?
3. What branches on your oak tree still have the opportunity to grow? Examples: gaining confidence, being assertive, developing interests, service to others using your talents.

Self-Care Tips

On the journey to wholeness and learning to love and respect yourself, it important to take good care of yourself. The bottom line includes a daily routine of getting proper rest, eating healthy food, and movement that suits your personality. Add to this taking good care of your body — your teeth, hair, skin. It is nourishing to choose colors that you like for your clothing and home furnishings. Next, you need stimulation to be personally challenged to grow and have interest in life. You also need people with whom to be close emotionally and with whom to share your journey. You need things to do that bring you pleasure and fun. Finally, you need a way to connect to yourself, such as daily meditation and contemplation.

A well nourished self meets life filled up. You have more energy to participate and give, to meet your challenges, and to do the inner work and self-healing required to have high self-esteem, good relationships, and enjoyment of your life. Take a look at the next page to give you more ideas of ways to nurture yourself.

Suzanne E. Harrill, M.Ed., Counselor, Teacher, Author: www.InnerworksPublishing.com

60 Ways to Nurture Myself

PHYSICAL	EMOTIONAL	MENTAL	SPIRITUAL
Take a walk	Deep breathe & think, "I am calm and peaceful"	Say an affirmation	Connect with Nature
Ride a bike	Share feelings about an experience with a friend	Read a book or magazine article	Concentrate on the flame of a candle
Soak in a hot bath with candles and music	Listen to music you like	Express your thoughts & feelings in a journal	Meditate
Exercise at the gym	Sing or make sounds	Make a "to do" list	Pray
Stretch and move to music	Hug someone, ask for a hug	Write a poem	Talk to your guardian angel
Practice Yoga postures	Pet your dog or cat	Write a letter	Listen to a guided meditation tape
Take a course in Tai Chi, water aerobics, or Pilates exercises	Talk to someone by pretending they are facing you in an empty chair	Listen to tapes	Write about your spiritual purpose
Sit in the sun for 15 minutes	Telephone a long-distance friend or relative	Email a friend	Visualize yourself in a peaceful place
Change one thing to improve your diet	Notice what you are feeling several times a day	List things you will do to improve your life	Do something of service for another or for your community
Watch birds and animals interact in nature	Write a letter to someone who has hurt you, but do not send it	Update negative beliefs that limit your life	Join a church group
Go swimming	Feel your fear and take a positive risk for change	Journal write daily about your reactions, thoughts, and feelings for a month	Learn about a religion different from your own
Sit in a garden or park	Smile at a stranger and send them thoughts of peace, acceptance, joy	List your traits, needs, and wants	Study with a spiritual teacher
Take a nap	Affirm yourself daily with self-nurturing	Make a list of short-term and long-term goals	Study ancient esoteric wisdom teachings
Get a massage	Watch children play, talk to your inner child in a loving, joyful way	Preview your day upon awakening. Review upon retiring	Practice unconditional love and forgiveness with self and others
Eat totally healthy for one day	Acknowledge yourself for accomplishments you are proud of	Work on your family tree	Practice a daily quiet time, a routine to connect spiritually

Add some of your own.

Suzanne E. Harrill, M.Ed., Counselor, Teacher, Author: www.InnerworksPublishing.com

I Am My Self

I am a worthy and precious being, an expression of Life. I am re-awakening to the inner knowing that I am whole and complete. I stop hiding from living and being my true Self. I unconditionally love who I am.

The next step in the greater plan for my life is unfolding much like a rose bud beginning to bloom. I accept with excitement the challenge and responsibility of going to greater degrees of awareness. I spend quiet time alone daily to listen to and trust the greater wisdom within me to unfold, guiding me in making wise choices that support my growth.

I accept myself right now, this moment, the way I am, even if there are things about me I do not like and want to change. As I grow in awareness, I discover ways to heal and release habits, traits, and patterns of thinking and behaving that do not support me, or reflect my true nature.

Inner peace grows daily as I forgive all people and events that have wounded me, including myself. I nourish myself with a loving support system that encourages me to take the risks I choose to take in order to grow and change. I accept their support when I stumble and fall, make mistakes, get confused, meet unbearable challenges, or stop my growth because of frustration or fear. I also allow them to celebrate with me when I reach mountaintops of striving and achievement.

I embrace each day as I live my life with ease, joy, awareness, and creativity. Resistance to what must be accepted melts away, as I gladly move forward to change the things I can as I play the hand I was dealt.

I love being who I am – My Self.

Note: These statements are good affirmations to write on your 3x5 cards.

Suzanne E. Harrill, M.Ed., Counselor, Teacher, Author: www.InnerworksPublishing.com

Lesson 3: Things You Were Taught That Are *Not* True and Things You Were Not Taught That *Are* True

I. **Warm up:** Take turns sharing with the group several things you like about yourself and something you are proud of that you do or have done. Discuss why it is difficult to talk about out good points. When is it appropriate to talk about accomplishments and when is it not?

II. **Thought Restructuring.** (Copy) Read and discuss.

III. **False and Destructive Concepts of Human Behavior.** (Copy) Read and discuss what the truth is for each. Remember Barksdale teaches all are false.

IV. **Limiting Guiding Beliefs.** (Copy) Rewrite as a group through discussion.

V. **Updating My Guiding Beliefs.** (Copy) Read the directions. Students may work individually or with a partner.

VI. **Self-Awareness Exercise.** (Copy) Pass out paper and demonstrate how to fold into quadrants. Read the directions. Ask the group to write their responses for quadrant one, Who am I? After most are finished ask them to write their responses for quadrant two, then three and four. Read out loud the questions for each quadrant as you get to them. Share in larger group.

VII. **Visualization.** (Copy) Read the introduction, lead the guided meditation including **Affirmations To Build Good Feelings** (Copy).

VIII. **Closing.** Share experiences from the guided meditation. Suggest that each person create a cassette tape at home to play daily to override negative self-talk. They may read the guided meditation on page 23 and affirmations on pages 24 and 25 or simply make an affirmation tape. Other affirmations may be used from earlier exercises, the self-esteem inventory, ones they make up, or ones from other books.

Thought Restructuring

"If you think you can. You're right. If you think you can't. You're right." Henry Ford.

Change your thoughts and you can change how you feel, which influences the choices you make. Thoughts form your belief system, the structure upon which you view the world. Many were adopted by you as a child and are not accurate; yet, they operate as your truth. Whatever you believe to be true, is true for you, even if some are false and limiting your experience of life.

Guiding beliefs are the rules that set your values, goals, choices, decisions, feelings, and behaviors in motion. Most are unconscious to you and many are assumptions and truths of unaware parents, teachers, older siblings, and the social norms during the time you grew up, that you accepted without question. Half-truths are handed down every day from parent to child or teacher to student that actually stifle the individual from feeling her/his innate value and potential.

To feel better about yourself, your relationships, and life in general requires a deep look at your inner structure to evaluate and determine which beliefs need upgrading to higher truths. Notice during our lesson today and for the rest of your life, things you were taught that are not true and things you were not taught that are true.

You have the opportunity to update some of your thinking in this lesson. Go at the pace that is comfortable for you. If some of the ideas are too big of a jump, simply consider them as possibilities. Take as much time as you need to evaluate these ideas before applying them to change your inner structure. Some of you may find it is easy to make shifts in your thinking. It usually takes time; however, to assimilate updated beliefs, even when you know they are beneficial.

Remember that you have the power and authority to determine what is right for you at this time as you update your inner structure. Know that results, such as higher self-esteem, will show up over time. The more you believe and feel your new thoughts, the sooner you will experience such changes.

Suzanne E. Harrill, M.Ed., Counselor, Teacher, Author: www.InnerworksPublishing.com

False and Destructive Concepts of Human Behavior[1]
By L.S. Barksdale

1. If you act "bad," you are "bad."

2. Winning is the only thing that counts. "Losers" and low achievers do not count.

3. You should feel guilty for your mistakes, defeats and failures, for you could have done better if you had tried harder.

4. It is wrong for you to love yourself.

5. You should be perfect – you should improve yourself.

6. Your worth is determined by how much or how well you do, compared with others.

7. You know better, so you should have done better.

8. You can validate your worth and justify your existence only through exceptional achievements, and the approval and acceptance of others.

9. Outside forces, circumstances, and the actions and attitudes of others, are responsible for your unhappiness and hurting.

10. Others have the authority and power to insult you and "put you down."

11. Self-indulgence and laziness are evidence of a weak will.

12. There are strong people and weak people. A strong person is one who can accomplish anything through a "sheer act of will."

13. Guilt is essential to motivate you to correct your mistakes and to do better in the future.

14. You should deny your own needs to serve the needs of others.

15. You must fulfill the demands and expectations of others because you need their acceptance and approval in order to be happy.

16. Your happiness depends on how much money, power, and prestige you manage to accumulate.

---

[1] From *Building Self-Esteem Instructor's Guide,* c1978 by Lilburn S. Barksdale and reprinted with written permission from the publisher and copyright holder: The Barksdale Foundation, P.O. Box 187, Idyllwild, CA 92549, Hwww.barksdale.orgH

Limiting Guiding Beliefs

Directions: Rewrite these common, limiting beliefs.

1. I never voice my opinion because it might make someone angry.

2. I must have love and approval from peers, family, and friends to feel okay.

3. I must be totally competent and almost perfect in all that I undertake. Mistakes are shameful and to be avoided at all costs.

4. I have a bad day when those around me are in a bad mood or when things do not go the way I want them to go.

5. I am a victim of my past (childhood, traumatic events) and I can't help that I simply react as events trigger my emotions.

6. I feel fear and anxiety about anything that is unknown, uncertain, or potentially dangerous, so I do not take many risks.

7. I need a partner to be a whole person.

8. It is selfish of me to want more out of life. It is wrong to be selfish.

Examples of updating these limiting beliefs.

1. I value my opinions and express my point of view when I choose, regardless of other people's reactions.

2. I value myself and let go of whether or not others are able to love and approve of me.

3. I do my best, correct my mistakes, and learn from them.

4. I allow others to have their moods and know my attitude is my responsibility. I plan my day, and flow as people and events change this plan.

5. I grow daily in my ability to respond rather than react. My past is healing.

6. I feel my fear and choose to take small steps towards what is right for me.

7. I am a whole person, with or without a partner.

8. I choose my needs over the wants of others, even if others label it selfish.

Updating My Guiding Beliefs

Write three guiding beliefs that no longer serve you. Write False over each. Next, rewrite each to reflect a higher truth that you now believe is true. Hint: think about past emotional reactions, or complete the statement, "Good mothers/fathers/wives/husbands/bosses/employees/always...," or look at **Possible Destructive Core Beliefs** on page 21.

1. _____

2. _____

3. _____

Add these updated guiding beliefs to your affirmation cards.

Suzanne E. Harrill, M.Ed., Counselor, Teacher, Author: www.InnerworksPublishing.com

Possible Destructive Core Beliefs[2]

ABOUT YOURSELF:

I don't deserve love.
I'm not important.
I must earn love to deserve it
I am not creative.
I am not lovable.
I am weak willed.
I must please others to be worthy.
I don't fit.
I'm not capable.
I'm not a worthwhile person.
My opinions aren't wanted.
My thoughts are dumb.
I'm a bad person.
Bad things I've done are not forgivable.
I can't do it.
I'm stupid.
I'm not as smart as others, so I'm no good.
I don't deserve pleasure.
I have to yell to get anyone to listen.
I'm boring.
It's bad to grow old.
I'm not respected.
I can't have what I want.
I'm not a loving person.
I must hide my true feelings.
I have to suffer in some way to receive love.
It's not okay to feel good.
I don't deserve happiness.
I'll never live up to my parents' expectations.
I can't live up to my self-image.

ABOUT THE WORLD

The world isn't a safe place.
The world is an unhappy place.
Life is unfair.
Life is hard.
Men/women are tough, scary, angry, etc.
People are out to get me.
The world owes me a living.

ABOUT RELATIONSHIPS:

I don't have what it takes to make a relationship work.
A relationship will only work with the right person.
I'll never find the right person.
If I love I will be hurt.
I'll get hurt if I get too close to someone.
All the good people are already in relationships.
I can't attract/keep a good person with my body.
I'm a loser.
I have to take what I can get.
I need my partner.
My partner can't get by without me.
She/he is just after my money.
Men/women only want one thing.
Women/men cannot be trusted.
We should enjoy the same things.
She/he should support me.
She/he is supposed to take care of me.
It is my job to improve my partner.
I have to protect/defend my partner.
It means something about me if my partner is attractive/unattractive.
She/he doesn't understand me.
She/he doesn't accept me for who I am.
What my partner says/does means something about me.
Relationships are hard.
Relationships don't last.
People I depend on will let me down.
The one I love will abandon me.
Divorce is a sin/failure.
I can't win so I might as well "get even."
I'm not meant to have a relationship.
Even if I try to explain, I won't be heard.
I must control my partner.
Marriage is a trap.
If she/he really knew me, she/he wouldn't be interested.
I have to be beautiful/handsome to be desirable.

---

[2] Reprinted from *Gathering Power Through Insight and Love* by Ken Keys Jr., and Penny Keyes, and staff. Copywrite 1987 by Living Love Publications.

Self Awareness Exercise

Take a sheet of paper and fold it in half and then in half again. When you open it there are four quadrants. Answer the following questions in each quadrant.

Quadrant 1: I am

Who am I?

Quadrant 2: I want

What do I want in life that I say I want, however it is not here now?

What would I like to be able to do?

Where would I like to go?

What talents or interests do I want to explore?

Quadrant 3: Blocks

What things block or stand in the way of me getting what I want?

Quadrant 4: Solutions

What do I need to do in order to move past the blocks and create what I want in my life?

What beliefs do I have that stop me?

Take turns sharing and discussing.

_____
Suzanne E. Harrill, M.Ed., Counselor, Teacher, Author: www.InnerworksPublishing.com

Visualization Exercise

Introduction: The images you see or sense in your mind are an important ingredient in creating your life. Just as you have an inner voice commenting all the time, you have images that continually picture your experiences. Some are helpful and others are not. The ones that manifest are the ones you hold strongly with feeling. Many people do not realize that these images are even taking place.

Anything you do starts as a possibility, with a thought or picture in your mind. Pretend you want to make spaghetti for dinner tonight and do not have all the ingredients. What does your mind do? It imagines when you have time to stop by the grocery store. Then your mind sees which aisles you must go down to pick up the two or three items. The same process works with creating a self-confident, risk-taking, self-actualizing individual. It may be a little more challenging if this is not in your current self-concept, because so much of your self-concept is held at an unconscious level where you simply repeat your conditioning. The good news is you can change the self-concept to reflect what you now know is true for you.

To feel better about yourself, you want to learn to be more in charge of your mind and the images and beliefs it sends to you. When you see or sense something in your mind's eye you add power to creating. Today we choose to be more in control of our mind so we can use it to support our continual growth into high self-esteem. Add your mental pictures with your affirmations to change more quickly. The more you can feel the images and words, the better for manifesting what you want. We will practice in the following exercise.

Guided Meditation: (Read slowly) Close your eyes and begin deep breathing. Gently affirm silently, three times, "I am peaceful and relaxed." Feel tension melt out of your body. Go to your place of peace, an inner place of safety and comfort.

Imagine something you want, such as confidence in speaking your opinions. See yourself achieving this. Deep breathe. Take a few moments to feel the enjoyment of accomplishing this new behavior with ease. See yourself able to pay the consequences, both good and bad, of this new freedom. Feel as if it is already true.

Imagine your future self speaking to you. Picture yourself believing and feeling as if these affirmations are already true. (Read the affirmations on pages 24 and 25.)

It is now time to open your eyes, move and stretch, and return to the room.

Affirmations to Build Good Feelings

1. I unconditionally love myself.

2. I am my own authority and accept the consequences, both positive and negative, for my choices.

3. I am accepting of myself when I make a mistake, using it to grow, change, and
become more aware.

4. I stop comparing myself to others, as I am one of a kind and incomparable.

5. I connect to my inner true self to feel good.

6. I set appropriate emotional and physical boundaries for myself.

7. I am responsible for my own life.

8. I allow people and events to "trigger" me in order to make peace with the past and to become more aware.

9. I give to the degree that I am filled up and get my needs met.

10. I stop being an emotional victim. If I do not like something going on in my life, I remove myself from people and situations not supporting my highest good.

11. I choose to develop and enjoy my interests and talents.

12. I am healing the pain and fear from the past in order to move forward with easy, joy, and creativity.

13. I stop value-judging myself and others.

14. I allow myself to feel.

15. I listen to the wisdom of my intuition.

16. I know I am doing my best at each moment based on my present degree of awareness.

17. I separate my behavior from the inner me; I am lovable even when I do not like my actions. All behavior makes sense when I look at the needs, both conscious and unconscious, motivating me.

18. I meet my needs with healthy choices.

19. I set realistic goals and expectations for myself.

20. I expand my awareness so I will have greater free-will choice.

21. I stop blaming and criticizing myself for undesirable actions, thoughts, and feelings. Instead, I take responsibility for new ways of living my life.

22. I build my awareness by seeing aspects of myself in the mirror of other people. Anything I notice, either good or bad, is a potential within myself.

23. I communicate with an intention of being authentic and genuine, letting go of double messages, game playing, and sarcasm.

24. I let go of expecting everyone to like, support, and agree with me.

25. I accept myself right now the way I am.

26. I accept everyone wherever they are in their level of awareness.

27. I forgive others who have hurt me from being unaware. Forgiving them does not mean I must have an active relationship with them.

28. I nourish myself with love from my spiritual Source.

29. I am worthy because I am alive.

Suzanne E. Harrill, M.Ed., Counselor, Teacher, Author: www.InnerworksPublishing.com

Lesson 4: Who's the Matter with Me

I. **Warm up:** Ask for success stories. How are you using this information?

II. **Self-Esteem – How Do We Get It?** (Copy) Read and discuss.

III. **Your Family of Origin.** (Copy) Read, answer the questions, and share in the larger group.

IV. **What Is Codependence and How Does It Affect My Life?** (The facilitator may do one of three things with this article: copy it for each student and read it aloud in class, give it out at the end of Lesson 3 to read as homework, or lecture from it.)

   Worksheet: What is Codependency and How Does It Affect My Life? (Copy) After you read or lecture, use the questions for group discussion.

V. **Questions and Answers: How Do I Change a Codependent Relationship?** (Copy) Read and Discuss.

VI. **Closing.** Ask everyone to share what they learned today? How can each see themselves using this information to benefit their life? Encourage students to write in their journals about today's lesson.

Recommended Reading:

Bradshaw on The Family: A Revolutionary Way of Discovery, by John Bradshaw

Homecoming: Reclaiming and Championing Your Inner Child, by John Bradshaw

Recovery of Your Inner Child, by Lucia Capacchionne

Books by Pia Mellody and Melody Beattie

Self-Esteem — How Do We Get It?

How does a sense of self begin? If self-esteem is how you feel about yourself and is influenced by what you tell yourself, where do these feelings and opinions begin? Your parents had the most influence on you as a young child. During infancy the mother or primary caretaker usually has the most affect. As an infant you had no emotional boundaries and only knew yourself as an extension of others, seeing yourself in the mirror of others. You were like a sponge, totally absorbing the early environment, including the thoughts, feelings, emotions, and awareness of those who took care of you. The way others related to you, talked to you, held you, and responded to you taught you how much you were valued. The relationship between your mother and father affected you on an emotional level too, as did their relationships with other members of the household. An absent or deceased parent affects a person too. Older siblings, relatives, and babysitters, also communicated their thoughts and feelings to you through their relationship with you. Like most children, you learned to value yourself to the degree you were valued by others.

Your early feelings about yourself were colored not only by how others valued you, but how much these others valued themselves. When a mother or a father loves her/himself, it is conveyed in words, tone of voice, and actions, so the young child easily feels and accepts the truth of her/his innate worth. Conversely, if a parent does not value her/himself, then the child picks this up as their own truth. Even if the words are "right," the incongruencies are felt.

When we live in a healthy family, the impact that parents have on their children is mostly positive. Remember that we are human and nobody gets it perfectly. The fact is, however, that many people have lots of problems, many of which are denied. These problems, patterns of thinking, and ways of being, get in the way of good parenting, so low self-esteem is perpetuated in the raising of children. The fastest way to build a child's self-esteem is for the parents to build their own self-esteem. Again, the way parents treat themselves is reflected to their children by their words and actions.

As you grew older, your peers and teachers mirrored aspects of themselves to you and further influenced you. A critical word or action deeply affects a young person. Words of affirmation are rare from peers and many teachers. Sadly, the lower the self-worth of a person, the greater the tendency to remember the negative and hurtful words, rather than the positive.

Other factors that contributed to your feelings of self-worth as a child were how well you mastered your physical and intellectual environment. Were you able to talk, walk, run, ride a bike, and catch a ball early or did you do these things a little later than your siblings and peers? When you started school did you already know your phone number, address, colors, and ABC's or not? Did you read naturally or was it a struggle? Then there is the impact of physical beauty. How attractive did others think you were and how did you feel about your looks? These early interpretations of physical mastery of your

body, intellectual development, and physical characteristics can affect your present feelings of self-esteem.

As a counselor I am optimistic about the ability to heal oneself of a traumatic childhood or toxic parents. The ideas presented in this course have helped many individuals who have made the decision to be proactive and improve their lives. I have learned much from people over the years too. Some people are survivors. They find ways to make it until they are grownup and can make their own choices to live life differently. Some of the ways people have helped themselves at a young age are to:

- have an imaginary family in their inner, imaginary world where they can retreat and pretend to have a comforting life
- spend lots of time out of the house
- adopt the family of a close friend to receive some kindness and support, as well as, observe possibilities to put into practice when they grow up
- create an imaginary friend
- connect with a spiritual helper outside of this reality (angel, spirit guide)
- develop a talent, such as performing well at a sport or being a good student, where acknowledgement is gained outside of the family
- read to either escape or to learn new ideas

Initially, positive experiences from others help a person build self-esteem. Exposure to healing modalities; such as, therapy, self-help books, or classes and workshops like this one, add to one's ability to do the things necessary to heal wounds to self-esteem. A person building self-esteem gets better and better at basing their self-worth on an internal sense of *okayness*, based upon a sound belief system of truth. Even though our childhood greatly affects us all, it does not have to stop us from having the life we want to live now and in the future.

Suzanne E. Harrill, M.Ed., Counselor, Teacher, Author: www.InnerworksPublishing.com

Family of Origin and Individuation

The family you grew up in conditioned you with their spoken and unspoken rules of behavior and thinking. These became your norm and silently rule your life today. You can choose a new path of autonomy and become an individual in your own right, evaluating for yourself the goals, values, beliefs, etc. that are right for you. To move beyond your conditioning and discover your true, authentic self, you need to separate from this system, evaluate it, take with you what is useful and of value, and release what is not serving you. Individuation was the term Carl Jung used to describe this life-long process, the unfolding of the essence of the individual.

In family systems theory, one idea that affects the individuation process is the emotional boundary rules learned in the family. On one end of the continuum is the enmeshed family system, which has weak emotional boundaries. It is difficult to know where you stop and another family member begins. If one person is in pain the whole family is in pain, individuals do not learn to feel their own feelings. In the extreme, there is not much privacy, as everyone knows every detail of everyone else's problems and business. There is little autonomy or independence, even in adolescence and adulthood. On the other side of the continuum is the disengaged family system. Here, no one interacts much; it is difficult to reach another for comfort, problem solving, or care. This is a very isolating system, with strong boundaries where members are on their own. The first family system is overprotective, smothering at times, and encourages dependence, while the second is under-protective, neglectful at times, and encourages independence, many times inappropriately. The healthy family system is in the middle, allowing such things as age-appropriate boundaries, autonomy, and privacy; as well as love, age appropriate care, affection, interest, and encouragement to grow and develop as an individual.

Answer the following with a partner. Discuss in the large group. Journal at home.

1. Describe your family of origin. Do you see it as more enmeshed or disengaged?

2. How much permission did you have to be autonomous, to make your own decisions, to be independent? Were you over- or under-protected?

3. Did you receive age-appropriate nurturing, support, and encouragement?

4. How are you repeating or reacting to these family patterns?

5. What did you learn about decision making and how does this affect you now?

What Is Codependence and How Does It Affect My Life?

Giving and helping people is a good thing and the world benefits when you go beyond self to help others. It's important to see what is going on inside of you, however, when you do give to others. Ask yourself what is motivating you and if it is healthy for both parties. We will look at codependence and learn to build better relationships.

Codependence is a new word that became popular in the 1980's. It has become a buzzword and, like self-esteem, is important for you to understand in becoming the person you want to be. In less aware times codependence was considered normal. To be good, perfect, compliant, agreeable, giving, and selfless was rewarded and was the unconscious standard with which many wo(men) were conditioned. Now we understand that there is a fine line between where being selfless and taking care of others crosses over to becoming a disease similar to having a physical addiction. If you want to have healthy, mature adult relationships with loved ones and close friends, you will benefit by understanding this condition.

What is codependency? Codependency is a term that grew out of the recovery movement and is what family therapists have termed enmeshment. This is when you are overly involved with another to the point of dysfunction. The codependent personality is formed while growing up in a dysfunctional family system which was emotionally repressive. The codependent does not have appropriate emotional boundaries, can merge easily with another, and does not experience the other person as separate from her/himself emotionally. If you are codependent, you go overboard responding to another person's problems, needs, and wishes before thinking of your own. To explain further, codependence is making choices about how to think, feel, or behave that are dependent upon considering the thoughts, feelings, and behaviors of other people before your own.

A Brief History of Recovery Movement

Now let us take a brief look at the history of the word codependent. The recovery movement began in the United States with Alcoholics Anonymous, co-founded in 1938 by Bill Wilson. He developed a peer support group to help alcoholics stop drinking based on twelve principles that changed his life. His spiritual awakening came as the result of practicing these twelve steps. To review The Twelve Steps of Alcoholics Anonymous, turn

to appendix I at the end of the book. At the end of this chapter I have included my rewriting of these steps for building self-esteem, which ties in with the theme of the last chapter.

As awareness of alcoholism grew, it was noticed that the partner of an alcoholic had certain types of behavior that were part of the problem. Early on they were labeled co-alcoholics, which was later changed to codependent. It was discovered that the partner had addiction problems too, but these were in the area of relationships with emotional addictions, rather than with a physical, chemical addiction to a substance like alcohol, nicotine, or marijuana. There was an unconscious investment of the codependent to enable the alcoholic to stay the sick, "bad" one with the problem, so they could be the good, helpful one, victimized by the chemical dependency of the addict. There was the need for the alcoholic to take the heat, so the codependent did not have to look at his or her own problems. As time passed it was recognized that you do not have to come from an alcoholic family system to develop codependence, this could also come from a dysfunctional family system. Since most families are dysfunctional to some degree, there are many codependent personalities in society that act out different degrees of emotional dependency addictions. Now we recognize that many people in our society suffer from codependence and many do not even know it.

Recognizing Codependence Characteristics

How do you recognize if you have a codependent personality or a tendency in this direction and need help healing this? If you are a caregiver, overly responsible, a dependent type person, do not like to be alone, are the rock your family leans upon, have made yourself indispensable to at least one other's functioning, need to be needed, are a people pleaser, or attract needy, dependent people, then you are a great candidate for this condition. A good rule of thumb to determine if your normal giving and interest in a loved one is dysfunctional and becomes codependency is answering "yes" to the following statements:

- I take care of you when you will not take care of yourself.
- I take care of you before I take care of myself.
- I foster dependency on me by doing what you need to be doing for yourself.
- I take care of your needs and do not take care of my needs.
- I check your thoughts and feelings before I know what I think or feel.
- Giving and receiving are not balanced in my adult relationships with family

members and friends.

Note: Here I am not talking about the care of young children, the elderly, the ill, or the challenged family member, with physical, emotional, or intellectual limitations. I believe you do have a greater responsibility in these situations to help people.

Fully-Functioning Adult

To be a fully functioning adult and have mature loving relationships with family members, you need to take care of yourself, your needs and wants, follow your interests, develop your talents, and have your own friendships outside of the family. You need to say "no" to doing tasks that foster immaturity and dependence in adult children; such as, buying, washing, or ironing their clothes on a regular basis. This strong boundary setting serves family members to separate from you, learn to individuate (be separate individuals), take care of their own needs, to grow up, and be able to have healthy, mature, adult love relationships. As you set limits on what you give, you foster family members and close friends to have mature adult-to-adult relationships with you. Here you relate in a balanced give-and-take way, where you are not in the role of being the "grownup" who is giving all the time. If you do things for your grown children beyond what is age appropriate, then you lower their self-esteem and actually stop them from growing up.

When you are codependent you are enmeshed with family members' emotional boundaries and you treat them as extensions of yourself. Therefore, you do not like to see them in pain, uncomfortable, making unwise choices, or unhappy. You like to "fix" them or their situations to be what you think is right and good for them. If codependency operates to an extreme, it involves subtle control over your adult children's choices of career, place of residency, choice of marriage partners, place of worship, and you generally dominate their decision-making abilities. Secretly you feel safe, secure, and loved when others need you and depend on you; it makes you feel important and gives your life meaning because you do not have your own life. There is little identity outside or beyond being the giver and, many times, the martyr.

Motivation

What motivates codependents to do this? Besides the overall comfort and security in being needed that can be experienced when others are dependent on you, the main reason is to avoid dealing with the painful feelings that are stuffed inside yourself. These might be

feelings of disappointment, unhappiness, trauma, abuse, victimization, lack of fulfillment, stagnation, and not growing and expanding toward potential. If you focus on another, then you can take your mind off of what has, or is happening, to you emotionally and you can stay in denial that you have problems that need attention. There is avoidance of the self. Since another's problems dominate your thinking, keeping busy with someone else's issues eases your inner discomfort, which keeps your emotions at bay. If someone is dependent on you and needs you, you do not have to look at your dependencies. There is a fear, usually unconscious, of no longer being needed. It starts in childhood where rigid, unhealthy rules dominated the family system.

Let us look at the dysfunctional family system briefly to see how many people have been conditioned to have emotional and relationship addictions, which create codependency. In a dysfunctional family, problems are denied and not discussed, and certainly you are not to discuss them with anyone outside the family. It is a closed family system where no new information or interpretations of situations can come in; so professional help is out. Therefore, you must stumble along pretending there are no problems, looking good to the outside world, but at the same time feeling the family problems and knowing at the emotional level that they are there. You receive no confirmation or data about what these problems are from your parents. As a child when you felt there were problems and the adults denied or ignored them, then you began to doubt what you thought and felt about problems not being addressed. Slowly you turned away from paying attention to your thoughts and feelings, becoming focused outside of yourself by *doing* instead of feeling. Many times there was a hidden belief that said, "You'll love me and pay attention to me if I'm perfect." You then may have focused on being a good student, achieving, giving, being good and not demanding attention, or being overly responsible, to name a few. As you practiced the family rule of denial, you stopped listening to your inner self telling you the truth about what you were thinking and feeling, and the awareness and growth process stopped. Eventually, the dysfunctional family system trains you to lose touch with who you are. You feel lonely, insecure, abandoned, and stop trusting your voice of intuition, as well as, other people. This carries over to adulthood.

Many times in the dysfunctional family, the adults have so many problems that the child's needs for proper psychosocial development are not met. At certain ages children

need more attention than at others. There is a fine balance between over- and under-involvement of a parent at each stage. Usually, when a parent is unaware and not willing to seek information from books or professionals, they do not know age-appropriate nurturing, safety, love, attention, or affection. So they over- or under-give to the child in each of the stages. When a child does not get dependency needs met, this contributes to emotional and physical dependencies, in adulthood, as does not getting independency needs met.

Developmental Process

Let us look at the developmental process of dependency in infancy to interdependency in healthy adult relationships. At birth everyone is totally helpless and dependent on adults to survive. It is very proper for a baby to need a lot of attention, holding, and responding to its needs and to depend on others. Trust is learned in the first year of life by how well those dependency needs are met. As the baby becomes mobile there is an important stage of counter-dependency. Here, with the safety of Mom or the caregiver nearby, the baby explores the environment, however, always making sure Mom is near. Eye contact is important here to convey interest and to send the message, "I will let you explore as long as it is safe for you and will set limits on what you do to take care of you." As you can see, it would be very easy to curb this natural curiosity to explore your world. If you are kept in a confined space like a playpen for long periods of time, or if Mom is so busy she does not give the constant reassurance of eye contact to you as a toddler, or if she overprotects you and hovers over your every move, you will not develop properly either.

There are degrees of independence that can be encouraged as a child naturally wants to do things for themselves and grow to be an individual separate from Mom. For example, a two-year-old wants to dress her/himself, even if it includes putting a shirt on inside out, wearing colors that do not match, or putting the shoes on the wrong feet. In healthy development the parent knows to let go and let the young child do many things for themselves, even if not done perfectly. What happens many times is the adult does not encourage this independence, which slows or even stops the desire of the child to be independent. Comments like, "Oh, let me do that for you. You are making a mess," are discouraging to normal independent development. The opposite can be detrimental also; such as, letting the two-year-old do too much, therefore, neglecting the child and not setting

appropriate limits on the independent behaviors. This can easily happen when the birth of the next child is close.

Somewhere around four years of age children figure out that Mom is not all knowing and all seeing. They figure out such things as, "If mom is not looking, I can cross the street and visit my friend." Here we have the desire to separate, to think and do things for self. Again, this has to be responded to sensitively, but this is basically a time to encourage the child to do much for her/himself. It is a good time for example, to allow the child to choose what to wear each day and to do some things without the caregiver watching every move.

The final stage is a little more difficult to teach, especially if we ourselves have not learned it. Interdependence is learning to balance between healthy dependency and connectedness in the family and relationships and appropriate independence of doing things individually. In a relationship or a group or a community there is always interconnectedness, and what you do affects me and what I do affects you, so a healthy respect for each others needs or of the members of the group is important. One needs to learn to balance ones own needs with the needs of the relationship, family, or community.

In a healthy family the parents model and teach their children interdependence. The children learn that sometimes it is appropriate to be dependent and get your needs met from the caregivers. While at other times it is appropriate to do things alone, to be independent and get other needs met, like exploring or being creative. Limits are put on total independence because living in a family or working in a group, we need to learn we can not only do what we want to do. The child needs to know when s/he has gone too far with independent actions and thoughts. When reaching a point of imbalance in actions, desires, or decisions s/he needs feedback when not being fair to others or not participating as a group member. Each child needs encouragement to play alone sometimes, to not participate with the group, or not be with the caregiver solely. At the same time each child needs feedback to come back and participate in the family or group when there is too much alone time. If too dependent, the child needs encouragement to take positive risks to move outside of the comfort level to explore. Aware parents also take into consideration the traits of each child. It is not a simple recipe that works for every person and family all the time.

Dependency and independence are both aspects of interdependence. When you do not have the proper nurturing at the proper time in early development, from dependency to

interdependency, then you get caught into the web of dysfunctional behaviors. Most of us have some problems as the result of this growth process, of not being parented optimally.

Good News

The good news is that you continue going through these stages and growth opportunities constantly appear throughout your life. That is why it is so important to recognize what was "off" in your upbringing so you can heal the wounded parts of your conditioned self. This is where the *inner child* idea comes from. We can re-parent the younger, immature parts of ourselves and heal our consciousness.

Besides our dysfunctional families and the parenting skills of unaware and sometimes mentally ill parents, there are dysfunctional belief systems that perpetuate codependence. One example is the religious teaching that says it is better to give than receive. This is a very high truth, if you are serving those less fortunate, less aware, or less able than yourself. It does not say it is better to give **more** than you receive when in an egalitarian, mature relationship. If you are dealing with a peer, spouse, or family member (exceptions young children and the elderly that cannot take care of themselves) there needs to be a balance.

Things get out of balance if you give out of proportion and match up with others who take out of proportion. This pattern draws people together many times in relationships. This lopsided energy exchange will make each feel victimized by the other person over time. The giver many times gives because there is a hidden expectation of receiving something – to be needed, a future favor, a pat on the back, words of endearment, or acknowledgment that one is a good or nice person, etc. When these "rewards" do not show up, the giver eventually feels taken advantage of and many times gets angry or hurt. The giving here has been conditional. In unconditional giving there is no expectation of a return and what you can give is given without resentment.

Interestingly enough, the receiver many times is not even asking for the things the giver gives. Many times the recipient feels that emotional and physical boundaries are being invaded and that there are hidden expectations to give something back. This person many times gets angry about being pestered and their space being invaded. Both the giver and the receiver are responsible for their part in the pattern. To make positive changes in a mature relationship requires both being honest and looking at unhealthy patterns that need to be changed.

Giving Is a Good Trait

Having the traits of giving and responding to others is usually a good thing. It becomes negative or codependent when you do not take care of your needs as well. You stop another's growth by giving what another needs to do for her/himself, or you ignore your own problems by helping others with their problems. There are healthy places to use the trait of giving to others. It is very simple. Give from your overflow when helping others. The degree to which you fill yourself up physically, emotionally, mentally, and spiritually is the degree to which you can give unconditionally. When your giving is unconditional and you think about what is appropriate for you and the other person, it is not codependent. It is the opposite. It is healthy giving found in interdependence.

The key to clear, clean giving and developing interdependence is to work on your own healing, beginning with learning what your needs are and meeting them. As you get to know yourself, you will learn to tune into yourself periodically throughout the day to listen to the needs of your inner self in order to find balance. Notice simple things such as whether you are bored and need people and more activity today, or you are tired, need less socializing and physical activity today and would benefit by being alone. If you need attention, admit it and look for appropriate ways to nurture yourself. If you need to be touched, you may treat yourself to a massage periodically. The main point is to take responsibility for your own nurturing, to get your needs and wants met daily so your giving comes from a good place. Stop giving time, attention, and emotional energy when you do not have it to give, which depletes you. Giving while emotionally needy or empty has a hidden agenda, a hook of an expectation of a return. Learn to heal the needy parts of yourself and to meet your needs. Identifying your needs may be the hard part. Again, as you spend quality time journal writing and pondering your life, you will discover your true needs. Talking to friends or professionals also helps.

On the journey to wholeness it is important to look at your patterns of giving to determine whether or not you are giving for the right reasons and actually helping others. At first it may be hard to be objective. Know that it takes time and the growth of your awareness. As you grow, heal, and learn to transform your codependency, you will responsibly give to others and have the privilege of truly being of service.

Suzanne E. Harrill, M.Ed., Counselor, Teacher, Author: www.InnerworksPublishing.com

What is Codependency and How Does It Affect My Life?

Use the following questions for group discussion.

1. Define codependency. 2. List Characteristics of someone who is codependent.

3. List ways giving becomes dysfunctional. 4. What motivates codependent behavior?

5. What in childhood promotes codependency? 6. What heals codependency?

7. How do you see codependency operating in your life?

Answers (Use these if class discussion needs a boost):

1. A codependent person has poor emotional boundaries and easily gets over-involved with another, giving or doing too much for that person. They concern themselves with the comfort or happiness of the other person to the point of losing touch with what is appropriate giving and what is right for themselves. Others are treated as an extension of self.

2. Some characteristics of a codependent: caregiver, overly responsible, dependent, is not in touch with own needs, does not like to be alone, is the rock of their family or work team, needs to be needed, people pleaser.

3. Five ways giving becomes dysfunctional:
    a. I take care of you when you will not take care of yourself.
    b. I take care of you before I take care of myself.
    c. I foster dependency on me by doing what you need to be doing for yourself.
    d. I take care of your needs and do not take care of my own.
    e. I check your thoughts and feelings before I know what I think or feel.
    f. Giving and receiving are not balanced in my adult relationships.

4. Motivation – to avoid dealing with the painful feelings that are within.

5. Some ways the dysfunctional family system fosters codependency are by denying and not discussing problems, not being open to help if there is a problem, having rigid standards and beliefs about such things as being good, not being open to new ideas that challenge the current beliefs, forcing children to grow up too soon or not at all, the language of feeling and intuition are denied which blocks communication with the inner self. Name some more.

6. To begin healing codependency begin building a relationship with yourself, build awareness, listen to your feelings, face your problems, get help with solving your issues, update your belief system, build your self-esteem.

Questions and Answers:
How Do I change a Codependent Relationship?

Following are some actual questions people have asked about codependent relationships. Use them to get you started thinking of your own questions.

Question 1: What do you do if you recognize you are in a codependent relationship and want to change it?

Answer 1: Go slowly. Begin opening communication with the other person to see how open s/he is to the subject and more specifically whether or not s/he is interested in learning about her/himself, as you are doing. Even if there is initial resistance, this does not mean the other is not willing to learn new patterns and heal a dysfunctional situation. Time will tell. If you have a willing partner/family member, share what you are learning about yourself, this course, the books you are reading, and how you wish to create a better relationship. Together you can take small steps to change the relationship.

If you do not have the okay from the other person, you need support to change yourself, which in time changes the dance between the two of you. You will have to take risks to put new patterns in place, such as setting boundaries, saying no, thinking of your own needs, or not being as available to the other person.

Question 2: I am a control freak. Am I codependent or is my wife?

Answer 2: Without knowing your wife, I would guess that you both are, since people match up with similar levels of awareness. You are for sure and the need to be in control and to control others makes you feel safe. It does not build warm, loving relationships, however. Nor does it allow others autonomy (to be a separate person from you) and to learn and grow from their choices. As you let go and allow others to make their own choices, both good and bad, and pay the consequences, you will help them mature. You will have to face your own insecurities, however, which are not evident when you spend all your time managing what others are doing and how they are doing it. As you manage your feelings and let go of control, you can grow into having better relationships with your wife and teenagers. Family counseling may be order. Others may not like your control; however, they may not be instantly pleased or begin to take responsibility simply because you stop controlling them. The patterns have gone on for quite a while.

Question3: I know someone who is codependent. How can I give them this information to help them?

Answer 3: Watch your own codependence. If you wish to impact others, live your truth and speak from your experience. If the other person shows interest then share more. Remember, continue to work on yourself.

Question 4: I see that I am in a codependent relationship. I am engaged and my fiancé likes to take care of me and do everything for me. I enjoy being taken care of; however, I see this is unhealthy.

Answer 4: Begin discussing you new ideas with your fiancé, as it is better to let him know your plans to change before you get married. The more you two know yourselves and each other, the less surprises after the marriage. The more you work on this together the better. You need encouragement to take small steps to do things for yourself. Your partner may or may not be able to do this at this time, so support may need to come from somewhere else. As you grow more independent, he will need encouragement to look at himself and figure out what to do when he is not being needed as much by you.

Question 5: I have known for a long time I am codependent and have not made much progress in changing. My partner is very dominant and I know I allow it. What do you suggest?

Answer 5: There are Twelve Step groups to help you, called CODA or Codependents Anonymous. Here you meet with people who have gone before you, willing to share their knowledge and to support you in taking the risks necessary to heal yourself, regardless of whether your partner understands or not. The emphasis is to work on yourself, the insecurities and fears that allow you to continue living unhealthy patterns. Awareness is the first step in change and then you need to take risks. Most people benefit from the support of others from a 12-Step group or therapy.

Lesson 5: Building Better Relationships

I. **Warm up:** Share success stories about using information in this course.

II. **Myths about Relationships.** (Copy). Take turns reading and discussing.

III. **Relationship Truths.** (Copy). Take turns reading and discussing.

IV. **The Three Stages of Love.** (Copy). Read and discuss.

V. **Relationship Realities.** (Copy) Read and discuss.

VI. **Keys to Long-Term Success in Relationships.** (Copy) Read and discuss.

VII. **Building Sound Communication.** (Copy) Read and discuss. Encourage each person to check off one or two things to focus upon this week.

VIII. **What Kind of Communicator Are You?**

IX. **Danger Signs in a Relationship.** (Copy) Read and discuss questions.

X. **What You Need to Know Before Saying "I Do."** (Copy) Read and discuss. How is this helpful to you or family members?

XI. **Journal Writing Assignment:** In class or at home write a letter to your partner or a family member expressing everything you wish you could say in person that never gets expressed; such as, what is important to you, what you like about the relationship, the things that you would like to change and improve in the relationship, what upsets you or past hurts that still bother you. The purpose is to gain clarity with yourself. It is not necessary, and perhaps not advisable, to give this letter to the other person until it feels right. If you determine it would be beneficial, you may need to rewrite the letter.

XII. **Relationship Enrichment Cards.** (Copy) In the Appendix II, page 71 is the master to create a set of cards for building intimacy with a partner.

XIII. **Closing.** What ideas impacted you today? Allow time for sharing.

Note: Choose handouts that meet the needs of your group.
Recommended Reading: 1. *Enlightening Cinderella* by Suzanne E. Harrill
                         2. *How to Keep the Love you Find* by Harvel Hendrix
                         3. *Why Marriages Succeed or Fail* by John Gottman

Common Myths about Relationships

We all have beliefs about relationships that are based on our observations of our parents, ideas society perpetuates, and personal experiences. Some are true and serve us and others keep us stuck expecting unlikely, if not impossible, outcomes. Following are some of the myths that some people have about relationships or the lack of one. Read the list and update them to a higher truth. Add some of your own.

1. There is only one person for me, my soul mate.

2. If only the right person would come along, then I will have the perfect, fulfilling relationship that I've been waiting for my whole life.

3. I married the wrong one.

4. I am waiting for love-at-first-sight to validate who the right partner is.

5. I have a perfect relationship with _____, but s/he does not ignite my passion, therefore I will keep looking.

6. This relationship is too hard, so I'm out of here.

7. If you have to work this hard to make it work, it must not be right.

8. I like most things about _____, but s/he is _____ or is not _____.

9. I am not going to fall for someone like my father or ex-partner.

10. I need a partner to be fulfilled. Two people make a whole.

11. I need the approval of my family to have a good marriage.

12. We have everything/nothing in common, so it will never work.

13. Even though I'm married, I am still looking for the right one.

14. You can't teach an old dog new tricks.

Relationship Truths

Relationships can not make us what we are not. For example, relationships can not make us happy. We have to learn to be happy within ourselves first.

Relationships show us our level of awareness, degree of maturity, blind spots, level of functioning, and our beliefs about ourselves and life through mirroring.

Relationships reflect how we are being and living in the world.

The foundation of a good relationship rests upon the most important relationship, the relationship with oneself.

As we trust ourselves and feel safe and secure, we attract trusting, safe, and secure relationships.

We love others to the degree we love ourselves.

No one completes us, as we already are whole and complete, spiritual beings waking up to this truth.

When we feel our wholeness and completeness we allow others to be themselves.

Control of others lessens and compassion grows, as we focus on our own lives, healing our issues, knowing and loving ourselves, and living creatively actualizing our talents, interests, and purposes.

To create a relationship we want, we have to live and be the qualities we want to attract.

To transform our current relationships to be more loving, giving, kind, vital, authentic, emotionally supportive, forgiving, compassionate, and intimate, we must become a match. We practice, live, and become more loving (which includes self-love), giving, kind, vital, authentic, emotionally supportive, forgiving, compassionate, and intimate.

The Three Stages of Love

Love grows and changes. The excitement that brings couples together in the beginning is very different from the love that emerges fifteen or fifty years later. Love relationships go through three predictable stages. All are important and none can be avoided if love is to mature.

Stage 1: Romantic Love
Love relationships usually begin with a strong physical and emotional attraction that produces an altered state of consciousness. Your brain is saturated with chemicals called endorphins, creating the sensations of intense pleasure that accompany infatuation. The exhilaration and sense of well-being are similar to feelings produced by vigorous exercise or eating something extremely pleasurable, like chocolate.

In this highly charged emotional state, you are apt to project images, expectations, and ideals of the perfect mate onto your partner. These projections often have little to do with who your partner really is, but it's hard to tell because both of you are on your best behavior. Reeling with romance and passion, you and your partner are highly responsive to each other. It is not until further down the path that you find out what a person is really like.

Stage 2: Power Struggle
As infatuation and romantic love subside, healthy relationships go through a period of adjustment with continuing power struggles. It is common during this stage, for each partner to try to mold the other into the ideal mate. As part of this process many couples bicker and fight. Some launch a "cold war" and start avoiding sensitive areas of conflict. If neither you nor your partner is ready to risk confrontation, your lives are likely to become more and more separate and devoid of intimacy and sharing. Even though you avoid open conflict, agreeing at some level not to argue and fight, the tension and pain remain. Here the problems go underground and come out when least expected.

Some couples use guilt and blame to control each other in an effort to recapture feelings associated with the earliest stage of their relationship. Both long for that period of infatuation when being together was new and exciting and the partner was attentive. If that sounds like you, remember that it's normal to fall out of romantic love and to experience conflict. Furthermore, confrontation is healthy. It builds understanding when you get things out on the table. Learning to confront and resolve conflict at this stage helps your relationship mature. The challenge is to discover what can be changed in the relationship and what must be accepted.

It is never too late to learn the skills and to take the risks to effectively move through the power-struggle stage in order to achieve a stronger more satisfying relationship. It requires honesty with self, the willingness to confront and communicate with the partner, and letting go of control to experience what needs to surface. This includes facing your fears and allowing all your feelings to be explored. Feelings are not right or wrong. When denied, however, anger turns to rage and playing "ostrich" to avoid dealing with issues turns to depression. (Healing these may require both inner work and therapy.)

Steering through the power-struggle stage can take years if a couple does not look for help outside of their frame of reference. There are some definite things a couple can do to speed up the process — gather information from books, take courses like this one, and go to counseling. Marriage and family therapists offer helpful information and objectivity when a couple is at an impasse.

Stage 3: Unconditional Acceptance
In its third stage, a healthy relationship moves beyond regular power struggles and control issues to unconditional love and acceptance. However, during the transition from stage two to stage three, partners must still confront and resolve issues in the relationship, taking risks to make positive change wherever possible and accepting those conditions that cannot be changed. Even in stage three, it is healthy to discuss anything that upsets you. Differences are approached positively, not seen as things to brush over, hide, or suppress. Tolerance and forgiveness are part of the equation, because there are always two different individuals with points of view, interests, desires, goals, and rates of growth.

At this stage, each person is highly aware of various traits in the other. Some you like and others you dislike, but you learn to accept the ones that cannot be changed. This is a time when expectations are readjusted and both of you become more realistic. Part of the process involves grieving the loss of expectations that cannot be met, and forgiving your partner for not conforming to your ideals. Making peace with yourself over the loss of your idealistic fantasies can take years — it really depends on your level of self-awareness, your willingness to let go of control, and the degree to which you are able to tune into the relationship. This third stage, acceptance, also includes enjoying the partnership and supporting each other on the journey of life to self-actualize and grow.

On the path to mature love, these three stages blend into one another. One does not stop and another begins. In fact occasionally, they all three take place simultaneously. For example, you can still create romance in the second and third stages. Remember the draw of the first stage, where there was the element of surprise and the unknown? To create some romance, change your routine and bring in the element of surprise and unpredictability. You might create a date night once a week, where you go out and do fun things together. Use your imagination. Likewise, during the third stage it is still important to bring up issues that get in the way of experiencing a good relationship. Communication is important in all stages, as is working on your own issues and building awareness.

Knowing these three stages helps people be realistic about relationships. Rather than giving up during the tough times of the second stage, it is helpful to know it is normal to have conflict and there are things you can do to make the way easier. Good relationships take time, awareness, risking, and good communication skills, to name a few, and require lots of practice. Each relationship is unique and incomparable.

Suzanne E. Harrill, M.Ed., Counselor, Teacher, Author: www.InnerworksPublishing.com

Relationship Realities

1. *Romantic love* feels good, yet is not a good predictor of long-term mature love. Its purpose is to get people together, to determine if there is potential for a deeper relationship.

2. When romantic love fades, the relationship moves to stage two, the *power-struggle* period. Here each becomes more honest with day-to-day living and can no longer hide shortcomings. It is common to project unrealistic ideals and expectations onto the other. Many people run from this stage or try to avoid it, not realizing that it is part of the path to building a genuine, satisfying relationship. Blending personalities, negotiating, and compromising take time.

3. Conflict is inevitable, regardless of how much love there is. Partners in good relationships learn how to resolve conflict. Confrontation is normal and even healthy when done with kindness and thoughtfulness. The sooner you tell the truth about what you are feeling and bring up issues when you feel hurt, taken advantage of, irritated, misunderstood, or ignored the better for the relationship. Suppressing them keeps you a victim, feeling angry and separate from your partner. Gentleness and good communication skills ease defensiveness in the partner.

4. Unfinished business from the past, including pain from childhood and earlier relationships, affects the current relationship. In stage two of a relationship, which can last for years, each projects earlier hurts onto the partner and the partner can easily trigger earlier pain. With aware partners, each learns to take responsibility for healing their own traumas and patterns of thinking and behaving, projections, and unrealistic expectations. As each one makes peace with their past and recognizes projections, the relationship improves and moves to stage three.

5. *Unconditional love and acceptance* is stage three of a healthy relationship. Here each knows the difference between what must be accepted in themselves and the other and what requires ongoing communication, on a day-to-day basis, for mutual benefit.

6. One person can positively impact the relationship by changing their own behavior and communication patterns. Healing one's past, building self-esteem, speaking from one's own experience with "I" messages, and dealing with feelings impacts the partner, eventually creating new patterns of relating.

7. Communication skills improve relationships. Begin with yourself. You can only communicate what you are aware of within self. Bickering and arguing results when couples do not know themselves. Journal writing is a helpful way to clarify thoughts and feelings, so you can be straight with your partner, letting go of double messages.

8. Many people look to relationships to make them feel happy, secure, or to be a whole person. Relationships have a special purpose that most people miss – to teach them about themselves. Rather than look for happiness from a partner or relationship, look within yourself. The degree to which you love yourself determines your capacity to recognize love and to be able to nurture love in others. Two people that learn to love themselves have a special relationship.

Suzanne E. Harrill, M.Ed., Counselor, Teacher, Author: www.InnerworksPublishing.com

Keys to Long-Term Success in Relationships

Introduction: Living with another person in a marriage or long-term relationship is one, if not the most, powerful way to know yourself, heal the negative effects of your conditioning, and create a happy, fulfilling life. How do you learn and grow from your relationships and at the same time create satisfying, successful relationships?

Many people marry for the wrong reasons: infatuation, happiness, dependency, to be taken care of, fill in missing pieces. Relationships are **organic**, however, always moving, changing, growing, and evolving. Choice based on anything static = disillusionment and dissatisfaction.

How do you marry your last partner first, live with one person for a lifetime, complete with partners who are not healthy enough and growing in your direction so you do not repeat patterns, or transform unhealthy, stuck-in-a-rut relationships to life-affirming, satisfying, conscious relationships?

The **solution** is the same in each situation; take personal responsibility for your own life — expand awareness, heal issues and negativity from your past, gather information to build new skills, take risks to transform unwanted patterns, become aware of what you want to create, and become conscious of your spiritual essence, your true Self. Practice self-inquiry and stay conscious.

Twelve Keys to Relationship Success

1. **Know Yourself** — Take a personality profile, study the enneagram. Observe yourself. Study your family of origin to understand patterns of thinking and behaving that conditioned you. What did you learn from your mother about love, communicating, anger, emotional support, money, relationships, happiness, personal development, etc? Your father? Are they true for you today? How have these impacted your relationship(s). Which need to be updated to higher truths?
2. **Love Yourself** — Expand feelings of self-worth and love for your partner grows. Review lessons 1 & 2 and mirror this to your partner. Accept your partner they way s/he is.
3. **Practice tolerance, patience, and forgiveness** — Your partner is in charge of her/his life, making choices and living according to what s/he values as important. When not meeting your wishes or needs, having traits you dislike, or making choices different than you would like, it is important to find ways to understand and accept your partner the way s/he is. People change for their own reasons not yours. Unconditional acceptance grows as you let go of control, release unrealistic expectations, and learn to value the other as is. Learn the difference between what has the potential to change and what you must accept about your partner and your relationship. Serenity Prayer.
4. **Resolve Conflict, Take Responsibility for Healing Your Own Issues.** — Differences arise in any relationship. Problem solving, compromise, and fair fighting techniques are necessary skills for living peacefully with another. Express yourself; communicate, know your limits, be fair, and be honest. Start by always telling yourself the truth about what you think and how you feel, then talk to your partner on a regular basis. Journaling helps clarify your thoughts and feelings before talking. Listen to your partner. Most people

want to be heard and understood more than agreed with. Recognize and do something about your personal issues that get in the way of a good relationship.

5. **Meet Your Shadow (Unconscious) Side** — Understand projection and mirroring. Projection is a psychological defense mechanism where you see traits, behaviors, or beliefs that you judge as bad or negative in others and not in yourself. The shadow includes good things you disown, also. To be a mature, fully functioning person, you need to claim 100% of yourself and take full responsibility for who you are and what you do. Allow your partner to be your mirror, reflecting traits, behavioral patterns, and beliefs that you have in common. The mirror can be a direct reflection or the polar opposite, as when one is neat and tidy and the other messy and disorganized. Both extremes deal with the same theme. Allow conflict that arises help you see more of your blind spot and where you "match" your partner. Notice what you like and dislike in others to show you unconscious aspects or potentials within. Read: *The Dark Side of The Light Chasers*, by Debbie Ford.
6. **Balance Personal Time with Together Time.** Independence is a good thing as is healthy dependency. Personal time includes such things as alone time, exercise or gym time, or being with friends. Together time includes activities with just you and your partner or when both of you share activities with others. When there are children, family time needs the same attention, including adults spending one-on-one time with each family member.
7. **Update Faulty Thinking** — Continue rooting out beliefs about relationships and life that stand in the way of your success and happiness. Update them to higher truths. Create affirmations with new truths to reprogram your subconscious mind; manifest new results.
8. **Have Fun Together** — Rekindle romance. What got you started in the first place? Find activities that you both can share, whether you are similar or miles apart in personality and interests. Have a weekly date night. Surprise the other with flowers. Tell jokes, laugh. Smile and touch each other daily.
9. **Build traditions** — Build roots and security. Celebrate birthdays, religious holidays, and holidays like the 4th of July with a yearly cookout with family & friends. Meet weekly for a dinner date, take vacations together, or attend a place of worship.
10. **Self-actualize** — Make choices to grow towards your potential. Develop your creativity. Build and use your talents, explore interests, learn how to get your needs met (many times without your partner), and grow spiritually. Support your partner to do the same.
11. **Take pleasure in what makes your partner feel happy** — Show interest and caring, love, and support for your partner's interests, work, hobbies, or volunteer involvements.
12. **Share Bonding Practices** — Build connectedness and oneness. Walk, meditate, or take a class together, drink coffee together each morning, share meals, talk daily before work or bedtime, express gratitude towards your partner and the relationship often.

To create and maintain long-term success in a marriage or primary love relationship, take personal responsibility for your own life and well-being, continue growing in awareness, allow your relationship to teach you about yourself, and practice the twelve keys to relationship success.

Suzanne E. Harrill, M.Ed., Counselor, Teacher, Author: www.InnerworksPublishing.com

Building Sound Communication

Good communication is like a circle where one sends and another receives a message. It fails if the message is not received. Approximately 10% of a message are the words spoken, 40% the tone of voice, and 50% the body language. Communication takes place on two levels; the **content level** which focuses on the words spoken and the **feeling level** where the real messages hide. Responding only to the words ignores the deeper, underlying meaning in a conversation.

Guidelines for Resolving Conflict & Fighting Fairly

1. Stick to the subject. Discuss one topic at a time. Do not confuse issues. If your partner attempts to change the subject, simply say, "That's important, but let's finish this first." Completing discussions produces feelings of satisfaction and closure.

2. Deal with feelings. If you or your partner get emotional, express feelings before problem-solving. Effective communication gets to the bottom of issues that may look insignificant on the surface. Recognize strong emotional reactions are a clue that something is going on beneath the surface. Anger, for example, may be covering other primary emotions, like, shame, rejection, fear, embarrassment, abandonment, or feeling controlled or "taken advantage of." Be a detective and ask yourself and your partner questions, such as, "What's really going on? What are you feeling? What's this bringing up from the past? What do you need that you are not getting?"

3. Take turns listening and expressing. Good communication requires that partners express themselves honestly and openly. Each has a point of view that requires respect. Hear what the other partner is saying even if you do not agree. When one person is talking, the other keeps quiet and listens without interrupting. Let your partner know what your heard.

4. Stay in the present. Express what you are thinking and feeling right now, even if the event you are talking about happened in the past or will take place in the future.

5. Speak from your own experience. No two people experience an incident the same way. Do not expect your partner to know what you think and feel. You are unique. You have your own history, conditioning, perceptions and beliefs. Take responsibility for yourself by using statements, such as, "I believe..., As I see it..., I feel..., In my opinion..., My experience is..."

6. Use empathic, active listening. Listen between the lines and look for meaning beyond the spoken words. When your partner is talking show caring and respect by making eye contact, facing your partner, nodding your head, or saying things like, "Yes, I understand," or "I don't understand, tell me more." Repeat what you heard. Use a supportive tone of voice.

7. Attack the problem, not the person. Avoid unkind personal comments, criticisms, or name calling. Agreeing with everything your partner says is not necessary, but hearing her/his side of an issue is. Respect your partner, even when you don't like what s/he says, thinks, or feels.

8. Find win-win solutions. After you and your partner have thoroughly discussed an issue, take time to look for creative solutions that are agreeable to both of you. Compromise is necessary sometimes, as is letting your partner's needs have a higher priority than yours at times. Honor your partner and do not attempt to dominate the solution process. It takes *two* to win.

Suzanne E. Harrill, M.Ed., Counselor, Teacher, Author: www.InnerworksPublishing.com

What Kind of a Communicator are You?

Directions: Which of the following basic personality types fit you? Usually we are predominantly one type, with a secondary one that also fits. Write or discuss with your partner how you see yourself. What are some of the challenges you have or have had in the past communicating with others. How might you do things differently? Can you match your style of communication with another's personality type? Share in the larger group.

1. **The Take-Charge Type:** Are you active, confident, decisive, independent, a problem-solver, organized, and punctual? Do you plan your day and the future and work well under pressure? Are you task/bottom-line oriented, usually in a hurry; and do you get impatient when another goes into too much detail and takes too much of your time? Are you dominant, a straight-shooter, a little too blunt and critical at times? Do you love freedom and get bored with routine? Do you see the forest rather than the trees and are you self-motivating? Take-charge types go from point A to point B in a straight line. Warm colors, such as red and orange, describe their active personalities.

    For others to match your style of communication they need to cut the chit chat, be specific, direct, not expect too much of your time, and speak in short sentences — "I need help," or "I disagree," or "Please tell me your schedule for next week."

2. **The People-Person Type:** Do you need people and relationships and like to communicate, relate, and share? Are you optimistic, warm and friendly, emotional, and almost always available to others, sometimes to the point of loosing track of time and not finishing tasks? Do you answer the phone as you are rushing out the door for an appointment? Do you smile and talk to strangers? Are you overly trusting and find it easy to open-up and become vulnerable, too quickly at times? Are you an easy-mark, a people-pleaser, and motivated by praise? People-persons go from point A to point B by impulsively jumping onto short side-trips or points of interest along the way. Light, warm colors, such as yellow describe their social butterfly personalities.

    For others to match your style of communication they need to chit chat before getting down to business, share a story, listen to you, allow for emotional reactions, direct the conversation back to the main point, and give you attention, support, and recognition.

3. **The Dependable Type:** Are you respectful of others, usually in a pleasant mood, loyal, cautious, patient, stable, slow-paced, and a good listener? Are you a great support person with a lot of stamina for completing things, giving a lot of hard work to a project (at work, home, family, or volunteer group)? Do you like to know what is expected of you ahead of time? Do you dislike change and prefer the status quo? Are you possessive at times? Do you have current pictures of the family? Do you like tangible motivators — cards on your birthday or expressing appreciation or a pay raise if your company is happy with your performance? Dependable types go from point A to point B in a curved or wavy line, like a wave. Blue is a good color to describe their calming, slow, gentle personalities.

   For others to match your style of communication they need to slow down, give you plenty of time to think, give you one project or idea at a time to complete or digest and be clear on priorities. They need to encourage you to speak up, give you tangible, concrete tasks and information, give reassurance, and show appreciation.

4. **The Detail Type:** Are you serious, analytical, accurate, task-oriented, and like freedom to work at your own pace? Do you need a lot of time to make a change, like to observe a situation before jumping in, only take calculated risks, work well alone and need encouragement to be part of the team? Do you dislike being emotional or vulnerable and need time to open up to another? Are you tactful, slow to respond because you like to think things through first, and a perfectionist who likes things orderly? Are you intuitive, overly sensitive at times, and prone to worry? Do notice details, seeing each tree instead of the forest? Are you suspicious of compliments unless they are very sincere? Detail types like to sit on point A for a while and decide whether or not to go to point B. Cool colors such as violet describes this steady-as-a-rock type personality.

   For others to match your style of communication they need to slow down; give you attention and sincere appreciation; notice details; not criticize your work (as you associate what you do with who you are); clarify priorities, allow you time to understand and if necessary repeat things; and give you time to think before responding.

Danger Signs in a Relationship

Some relationships are not able to grow through the power-struggle stage to emerge into a mature loving relationship. In fact, this second stage may reveal severe dysfunction that prevents trust, commitment, and intimacy, thus sabotaging the relationship. There are no perfect relationships; most have places that need attention and have some degree of dysfunction. Some relationships cross the line, however, and are even harmful. Professional help may be needed. What are some early warning signs of real problems, not simply the normal growing pains of the power-struggle stage?

Some danger signs are when one partner in a relationship:
- threatens to use or does use physical force or violence to control the other
- is easily enraged and has a short emotional fuse
- is a rigid "black or white" thinker with no shades of gray (things are either right or wrong)
- has no respect for boundaries (violates other's emotional or physical space)
- lies
- is unable to take responsibility for her/his part in a power struggle, projection on partner
- is overly critical and domineering; will not listen to a different point of view or compromise
- continually projects her/his issues on to the other and has distorted perceptions
- feels overly jealous or envious to the point of being paranoid (accuses and imagines things that are not true)
- has long-term unresolved authority/power or mother/father issues
- is neglectful to self or partner
- has double standards for self and partner
- does not respect or honor spoken and unspoken rules of the relationship
- has very low self-esteem
- has a drug or alcohol abuse problem or has an untreated addiction or mental illness
- add some more

Each of us must decide what is right for her/himself when problems are evident. As discussed in previous lessons, we base our decisions on our level of self-esteem and guiding beliefs, many times living other people's value systems and obeying "should messages," rather than thinking for ourselves. Look at your beliefs and values as you answer the following questions.

1. How does this list of danger signs affect you? What comes up for you as you read this list?
2. When is a relationship too dysfunctional to progress into a mature relationship?
3. Should a person stay married if there are too many danger signals and achieving a mature loving relationship is unlikely? Why? Where did you learn this?
4. How does a person know how long to tolerate a bad relationship or know when to leave?
5. What degree of dysfunction have you tolerated or do you tolerate and yet know it is "right" to stay in a relationship? What allows you to stay? When do you get professional help?
6. From this discussion, are you aware of anything on which you need to take action?
7. Express anything else you would like to that this brings up for you.

Suzanne E. Harrill, M.Ed., Counselor, Teacher, Author: www.InnerworksPublishing.com

What You Need To Know Before Saying "I Do"

Investing in the stock market is a better risk than getting married these days. The 1998 Census Bureau Report found that between 1970 and 1996 the number of divorced people in the U.S. more than quadrupled. Current statistics show that more than 50% of first-time marriages end in divorce, and it is even higher for second marriages. Of those who stay married, many say they are not happy. What's wrong and how can you beat the odds to live happily ever after?

Many people have a fantasy that says, "If only the right person would come along, then I will have the perfect, fulfilling relationship that I've been waiting for my whole life. I will recognize my love-at-first-sight prince (princess) by the way he/she ignites the spark of physical desire within me." What is wrong with this belief, besides the obvious fact that there are no perfect people, is that you always have to live with yourself, including negative behavioral and thought patterns learned from your family and society when growing up. So don't be surprised that when the newness of the relationship wears off, your partner may not look so perfect, and may even start reminding you of traits you didn't like in your mom or dad or a character on that favorite TV sitcom.

What should you do then? End every relationship that reminds you of your past? No, because no one would ever stay with a partner for long if that were helpful. Instead, learn the truth about building a satisfying, long-term relationship. It begins with knowing yourself, understanding the stages that relationships go through, and learning skills to improve problem areas in your life; such as, assertiveness or good communication patterns.

The first thing you should know before saying "I Do" is that you will be attracted to people that help you heal unfinished business from the past. In other words, as issues you could not resolve with mom or dad (or siblings, ex-partners, etc.) come up in the current relationship, you as an adult now have the opportunity to handle things differently. The good news is that the more you know yourself, the better job you will do matching up with a partner with whom you want to heal these patterns. This includes finding a partner who is willing to know her/himself as well.

Now let us look at seven common mistakes people make in choosing a life partner that lead many to later disappointment or divorce. Mistakes people make include:

1. **Thinking physical attraction is a good predictor of a lasting relationship.** Wrong. Meet all parts of the other before assuming that feel-good sensation of "chemistry" between you two is love. While dating, be a detective and observe how the other's values, habits, preferences, beliefs, goals, and personality traits fit in with yours. Many people make the mistake of falling head-over-heels for someone they barely know and need to remind themselves that infatuation is not true love. The solution is to assume there is much more to a person than what meets the eye during the first six months of courtship. Getting to know someone on a deeper level than just the

physical takes time. This is time well spent and improves your odds of having a lasting relationship.

2. **Believing that when romance fades the relationship is ready to end or is doomed to unhappiness**. Wrong. Mature relationships move past the infatuation of the first stage to build something deeper — a relationship supporting growth, healing, fulfilling goals, commitment, and responsibility, to name a few. It includes living with a person who cares about you and wants to travel with you through the twists and turns life will bring.

3. **Assuming you can change what you do not like in your partner once you're married.** Wrong. People change when the motivation comes from within. Most do not easily or willingly change just because their partner wants it. Think about the effort it takes to change one of your own habits or personality traits. It is naive to assume your partner will change in the ways you have in mind. Unrealistic expectations set you up for disappointment. It is normal to not like everything about your partner, but do pay attention to how much you do not like the other person's habits, beliefs, values, goals, etc. If there are too many things you do not like, consider that person may not be a good match for you. On an up note, people change when we change ourselves. To instigate improvement in your relationship, change your dance steps and your partner has to change his/hers, or there is no one to dance with.

4. **Thinking power struggles mean the relationship is not a good one.** Wrong. The second stage of relationships is a power-struggle stage, where two different personalities work out how to live together. It is a disappointment to many after the romantic first stage, because reality has set in and it takes a lot of dedication to workout your differences. Learning good communication skills helps you move beyond pure arguing to fighting fairly to resolve conflict and to problem-solve. The sooner you face the power-struggle stage, the sooner you move onto the third stage of a relationship, the unconditional love and acceptance stage. Here you know the difference between what must be accepted in the partner and what can change. The part that can change requires continual communication and negotiating on a day-to-day basis to maintain a healthy relationship.

5. **Believing confrontation is not a good way to communicate**. Wrong. Confrontation is normal and healthy and does not have to be done aggressively. It is simply telling the truth about what you are feeling, thinking, and needing. The sooner you bring up issues when you feel hurt, angry, taken advantage of, irritated, misunderstood, or ignored, the better for the relationship. Suppressing them keeps you a victim and only leads to hostility and feeling separate from your partner. It is well worth the risk to face your partner with what is on your mind. It builds trust when both partners tell the truth about what they are feeling, thinking, and needing.

6. **Thinking it is too late to call off the wedding once the date is set**. Wrong. Listen to your inner self. If your body or intuition tells you that something does not feel right,

honor this and slow things down. It is wiser and less complicated to call off a wedding than to set yourself up knowingly for an unhappy marriage or to go through a divorce further down the path. A good rule of thumb is to date for more than a year, so you have a chance to see each other's shadow side and so there will be no major surprises. Remember this choice affects you the rest of your life!

7. **Feeling that counseling is a sign of failure and only for disturbed people.** Wrong. Failing to get help when there are problems is a missed opportunity. Most people do not like to admit they need help when things take a difficult turn, but research shows that premarital counseling increases the chances of a happy marriage. Why not let a neutral third party (like a therapist, minister, or rabbi) help you see your blind spots, your partner's blind spots, and clarify who needs help with the issues. Besides providing insights and encouraging you both to talk, counselors educate you about the basics of good communication and fair-fighting skills that most people never learn growing up.

Finally, let's look at building a strong foundation before making the life-long decision of choosing your partner. The truth about building strong lasting relationships is to:

1. **Know yourself**. Take an honest look at your traits — strengths and weakness, your goals, your values, your self-esteem, how you handle your anger, and how you nurture yourself, to name a few. Learn where your blind spots are, so you can build your awareness. Gather information when you need help. In areas where you are weak, get help. Find a teacher or counselor, begin reading or listening to tapes, observing others who know this skill better than you, or taking classes or workshops on the subject.

2. **Love and accept yourself**. You can only experience love to the degree that you love yourself. The degree of love, acceptance, and respect you have for yourself is reflected to your partner, and vice versa. By nurturing yourself physically, emotionally, mentally, and spiritually, you grow in your ability to love and honor yourself, thus impacting the relationship. When two people value high self-esteem, the relationship is set on a solid foundation.

3. **Learn as much as you can about your family history**. Did you know that the less aware you are of yourself and your family history, the more likely you are to repeat the same problems your parents and grandparents did in their relationships? People who understand their family patterns do a better job healing the issues that come up in a relationship, vowing to do things differently.

4. **Think about what you want in a relationship.** What do you picture in a good relationship for you? What do you see in your future? In five years, ten years, a lifetime? If you don't know what you want, you may end up with what somebody else wants for you. Empower yourself by discovering what you want to create and experience.

5. **Get to know your partner.** Be a detective and find out as much as you can about him/her and his/her family of origin. No one is perfect, but you can make wiser choices in choosing a partner by using your head **and** your heart.

6. **Discuss openly with your partner all of the above**. When you invite your partner to participate on the self-awareness journey, you have an almost sure bet of building a mature, satisfying, long-term relationship. Remember you are looking for someone with whom you want to do the dance of life, someone who will work on his/her issues as you are working on yours. Growing couples have an alive, caring, actualizing relationship.

Now you know how to live happily ever after. Improve your chances of a happy, long-term relationship before you say, "I do." Take the time to expand your awareness about yourself, about your partner, and about relationships in general. Then **choose** the right partner by asking yourself, "Is this the person I wish to learn and grow with as I go into my future?" **Beat the odds and marry your last partner first.**

Suzanne E. Harrill, M.Ed., Counselor, Teacher, Author: www.InnerworksPublishing.com

Lesson 6: Spiritual Growth: Developing Deeper Meaning and Purpose in Your Life

I. **Warm up:** Share feelings about endings and this being the last class.

II. **Introduction:** On the journey of self-discovery, inner healing, and self-empowerment, the need to look for deeper meaning for one's life surfaces. The desire to understand one's self in relationship to the bigger picture, to take more personal responsibility for one's life, to make sense out of unplanned events, and to feel a deeper connection to all of life become important. Asking questions like, "Is this all there is?" or "Who am I?" or "What is my purpose?" begins a deeper search.

III. **Writing Your Mission Statement.** (Copy). Read directions and examples, do exercise. Discuss how this impacted each of them. Encourage participants to rewrite as awareness grows after completing the Life Purpose Inventory.

IV. **Stages of Moral Development According to Piaget and Kolhberg.** (Copy) Read and discuss. Where do you see yourself? Others in your life? Notice the two major categories, external and internal motivation, and how these tie into low (external locus of control) and high (internal locus of control) self-esteem. Can one be in two different stages at the same time?

V. **Personal Integrity Builds My Self-Esteem.** (Copy). Read, pass out paper. Ask each to choose one value, then answer each column. Ask them to share.

VI. **This Can't Be Happening to Me! Disappointment, Loss, and Grief** (Copy). Read and discuss. The questions are good for journal writing later.

VII. **Finding Your Life Purpose.** (Copy). Read or discuss in your own words.

VIII. **Life Purpose Inventory.** (Copy) Pass out paper. Choose one or two items on the list to write about for 10-15 minutes. Ask for sharing.

IX. **Guided Meditation.** Read to the group, including **Affirmations for Inner Healing.** (Copy). Afterwards allow time for sharing.

X. **Closing:** Take turns sharing how the course impacted each and what endings are like for each. Encourage people to continue friendships.

Writing Your Mission Statement

Answer the following questions quickly with the first things that come to mind. If you start thinking too much, skip to the next question and then go back to skipped items.

1. What gives your life meaning and a sense of purpose? _____
_____
_____
_____

2. What situations, people, or events catch your attention, stimulate, and catalyze you?
_____
_____
_____

3. What is important to you? _____
_____
_____
_____

4. What would you like to accomplish? _____
_____
_____
_____

5. What is your highest purpose? _____
_____
_____
_____

My current mission statement is:
_____
_____
_____

(rewrite as you gain more clarity)
_____

Suzanne E. Harrill, M.Ed., Counselor, Teacher, Author: www.InnerworksPublishing.com

Examples of Mission Statements

To know myself and help other people.

I, (Your Name), choose to live my life with awareness and in community with other people, doing my part to create a better world.

I, (Your Name), want to bring more love and peace to the world by working with the Hunger Project in my spare time.

I choose to use my talents by working with adolescents in recovery.

To add peace to the world by healing myself and my relationship.

I plan to live each day to its fullest, to notice simple things, connect with other people, and to nurture myself on all levels. I choose to pass on to others a step behind me on the path of life things that are helpful and that I know are true. I want to help eliminate mental suffering and feelings of separation and isolation on the planet by spreading seeds of Truth.

I want to be the best manager I can be at work, mentoring those who work for me, modeling high standards of excellence and ethics, and creating a loyal team of productive employees.

I live being my true Self.

Stages of Moral Development According to Piaget and Kolhberg

The spiritual life passes through definite developmental stages. Not many people reach the highest state: that of fully internalizing moral principles. These stages are not easy to describe precisely. Each reflects a combination of ideas, attitudes, and decisions that represent a portion of the broad spectrum of spiritual growth. When working to raise the level of moral development in yourself or another, begin to work with information that is one step ahead of where the person is operating at the present time.

External Motivation — The motives for action are outside of one's self.

Level 1. The motivation is pain or pleasure which someone or something gives one.

    Stage 1. People act out of fear of punishment.

    Stage 2. People act because they are seeking a reward or pleasure.

Level 2. The motivation is conformity or conventionality.

    Stage 3. People do things because they want others to think well of them, to accept them.
    Stage 4. People do things because of the law. They follow the law and maintain it, but accept no responsibility for it.

Internal Motivation — The motives for acting are one's own. Responsibility is accepted. One comes from the heart in making decisions.

Level 3. The motivation is an internal principle by which one judges and determines one's actions.

    Stage 5. People begin to be involved in making decisions for themselves. They accept personal responsibility and make personal commitments. This is the contractual stage, in which people still see the need for law; however, it is no longer absolute. They believe it can be changed in certain circumstances and that their behavior is guided by contracts they make with others.

    Stage 6. People live out their principles. The central principle is that of justice and love, which directs all their actions and influences their ideas and attitudes. Belief and action become one.

This handout was created by Sister Carmalita at Nicholls State University, Thibodaux, LA.

Personal Integrity Builds My Self-Esteem

Integrity means being honest, sincere, and of sound moral character. To develop into a mentally, emotionally, and spiritually whole person it is important to live from your value system. For example, when you value being trustworthy, being a person of your word, loving unconditionally, being honest, or being nonjudgmental, it is important for you to live from this personal moral code which improves how you evaluate yourself. When you miss the mark, it can cause you to feel disappointment, shame, guilt, and self-loathing. When you strive to live by the values you hold important, or that you expect from others, it builds your self-esteem.

Assignment:
For the next 60 days do this assignment in your journal. You can add to it and review it for the rest of your life. Make four columns on your page. In Column 1, begin identifying your values and list them. In Column 2, be honest with yourself and write down examples of ways you have or do violate your value system. In Column 3, write a course of action to build integrity with yourself. In Column 4, write down your results: successes and failures. (A friend received this exercise from his AA sponsor years ago.)

Over time this exercise adds to your awareness as you make positive choices to heal your life. Be good to yourself and do not use this exercise to continue putting yourself down. All change begins with intention, the intention to do better day by day. Striving to improve your personal integrity can actually become one of your values.

Example:

Column 1	Column 2	Column 3	Column 4
My Values	Ways I have or Do Violate My Values	Course of Action	Results: Successes and Failures
Being Nonjudgmental	I criticized myself yesterday when I weighed myself.	Either I do not weigh myself after eating sweets or say positive affirmations to myself before I weigh myself when I have eaten too many sweets.	I was kind to myself when I chose not to get on the scale even when I suspected I was heavier.
	I judged my friend in my mind when I learned she went back with her boyfriend.	Talk to myself about allowing each person to learn their own lessons and about looking at my own issues.	I felt less angry with my friend when I met her for lunch yesterday. I still had to keep reminding myself it was none of my business.

This Can't Be Happening to Me! Disappointment, Loss, and Grief

When asked to describe the most wonderful future he could experience, a client named Ron answered, "I want to be happy like I was before I lost my job." I replied, "I want that for you or something better." He eyed me curiously as if to ask, "What is the something better?" His look told me he was ready to make peace with his seven-year cycle of disappointment, pain, and suffering. When faced with disappointment or the loss of something we hold dear, it throws us into a process of grief. When we do not ask for the experience, we often feel victimized by the things beyond our control that force us to change. One who has gone through the grieving process and completed their grief has a deepening of character; much like steel that is heated and then put into cold water. The forging makes the steel much stronger.

Ron is no longer innocent and arrogantly pushing through life as he once did. He knows, from the experience of loss, that he is vulnerable and that life is a very precious gift. He looks in more directions now to enjoy his life. It can never be taken for granted or be the same for him as he had once hoped, but it does not have to be negative. Even though it is different, he is learning to discover deeper meaning and purpose. His spirituality and connectedness to others has a higher priority now. As he makes choices for his future, he has the humility to know he co-creates with others and the hidden forces, as he calls God.

Life forced a process on Ron that was not to his liking. It could also have started with a divorce, a move to a new place, the death of a loved one, or a teenager acting out. It could be having to face drug or alcohol problems in self or a family member, the betrayal of a partner, learning of a life threatening illness affecting one's self or family member, the process of aging, or simply having unreal expectations. Eventually, it happens to us all. These unexpected experiences shift our lives away from our beliefs of "how things are supposed to be." It is part of the human experience, yet many of us are ill prepared to handle grief or know how to complete the grief process.

Our busy, fast-paced, high-achieving society provides little support or accurate information to help us deal with loss. We have learned to have a stiff upper lip, ignore our feelings, and believe that if we do express emotions, we should act as if we are fine as soon as possible. Not only do we hide our emotional pain from others, but we deceive ourselves, many times, because we think we "should" be over it after a certain amount of time has passed. Unresolved grief can go on for years if we do not complete our grief.

An important part of the grieving process is to admit that there were both good and bad aspects about the job, relationship, etc. before the loss. The job, person, or relationship was not perfect and we have lots of feelings, especially about the negative aspects. Ignoring our negative feelings keeps us stuck in glamorizing the past. Sometimes we think the only way we could ever be happy again would be to go back to the past and get the old job or relationship back. To help ourselves enjoy our present life, we need to complete our grief. Taking a seminar on grief recovery, working through issues in therapy, or reading good books on the subject can help us. (Three books on the subject are listed at the end of this article.)

No one grieves in exactly in the same way; however, it is helpful to know what some have experienced. Even with a necessary loss, such as leaving home as a young adult or a divorce of

choice, one might experience such things as appetite loss, lack of energy, little interest in exploring new things, and isolating one's self from others. Dr. Kubler-Ross gave one model of stages one goes through when experiencing death and dying: denial and isolation, anger, bargaining, depression, and acceptance. Again, everyone grieves differently, so if you do not experience all of these stages it is okay. The important thing is to go through the process of grieving so you can again enjoy a life with meaning and purpose. It is important to feel and express your feelings and to accept the help of others. Eventually, it is healthy to take the risk of engaging in life and not isolate yourself.

Ron, like others in the grieving process, was "pushed" to feel the full range of human emotions: disbelief, denial, anger, shame, disappointment, fear, and sadness after the loss of his job. At first all that mattered was to stop these intense feelings and return to what once was. His curiosity at my "something better" statement, along with his readiness to hear me, helped him move out of the stuck place of not finishing his grief. He was ready to make peace with life and, eventually, to feel thankful that he was a very different person now after having gone through the experience of losing his job. He realized that there might be something deeper going on and he was ready to move forward to a very different future than he originally thought would fulfill him. Before the experience of losing his job, Ron lived in a small, ego-driven world, believing all was well; he had no desire to actualize his hidden potential or learn things that would broaden his horizons and enrich his life.

Life is so much fuller for him now. His world continues to grow as he looks for deeper meaning and purpose when things do not go his way. Ron is learning to catch himself when he starts placing too much emphasis on his current job, which, by the way, is in an entirely different field. Once he got to know himself better, he could make choices better suited to his personality, interests, and talents. And Ron admits he likes himself better too. His relationships with his wife and children have also improved with his change of priorities. The job loss seven years ago inspired this new level of awareness. He wonders sometimes where he might be if he had not suffered this loss.

On the path of life it is much easier to make changes, to let go of people, jobs, behaviors, and ways of thinking when we choose the process consciously. The motivation is high when we choose to explore the self, build greater awareness, heal our past, and seek to express our potential. Even if taking risks is difficult, we are motivated because it is a choice. When the process comes unexpectedly and is not a conscious choice, the motivation to change is often lower. The latter is usually a sudden, shocking experience and we feel overwhelmed by the surge of feelings and often resist the direction our future now must take. Eventually, we must learn to surrender to the process of loss and grief in order to come to terms with the changes in direction that our life takes. Doing so enables us to reach the place of acceptance and deep peace where we are open to experience "something better."

Recommended Reading:

1. *The Grief Recovery Handbook* by John W. James & Russell Friedman

2. *Good Grief* by Granger E. Westberg   3. *Necessary Losses* by Judith Viorst

Grief Recovery: Journal Questions to Get You Started

1. What are some of the losses you have experienced in your life? Think about the times in your past when you were hurt, disappointed, or someone died or left you.

2. Write about one that still bothers you today. Eventually write about other losses.

3. What did you do to help yourself cope with the loss? Was it helpful? What would you do differently today with your present awareness?

4. Express feelings you still have about the situation. Include positive, as well as, negative feelings.

5. What did you believe to be true about the situation then? and now?

6. What is difficult to accept, resolve, or make peace with? What is your hunch about what will help you do this? If you feel stuck would you be willing to further your grief recovery with a seminar, counseling, or further reading?

7. What else do you want to say about disappointment, loss, and grief in your life?

8. Share what you have written with a trustworthy person or group where you feel comfortable.

FINDING YOUR SPIRITUAL PURPOSE

Are you ready to take the next step, now, to find your spiritual purpose? Do you know yourself pretty well and have you worked on inner healing? Have you begun asking questions; such as, why am I here, what is my spiritual contribution to the world, or how do I tune into divine guidance to direct my life? These and many other questions will surface when you are ready.

To begin the process of discovering your special mission, the questions on the Life Purpose Inventory will help you get started. Ignore any negative self-talk that wants to stop your inner guidance by telling you that you are not capable, smart enough, evolved enough, or worthy enough to participate in life in a larger way. Remember this is a process and it will take time to weave together the tapestry of your higher purpose. Honor the proper timing for you.

Writing in your journal is an important part of this process. It records your thoughts, feelings, and impressions so you have easy access to the information gathered over time. If you answer the questions today and find yourself getting more information during the next few days, continue writing or answer the questions several times. These questions require quiet time, so answer them when you know you will have time alone. You may choose, for example, to get up early for the next couple of weeks to write. Write down messages, impressions, suggestions, hunches, or feelings you receive from your dreams and daydreams during this period.

After answering the questions on the next page, meditate and ponder your answers. Continue to journal write daily until you feel a sense of direction or clarity. You may sense the part you are to play and the arena in which you will play in the big picture of life or you may simply see the next step or two for you. Write down all your impressions, as they are important even if some appear to be mundane; such as, getting your house, closets, drawers, or files in order. Once you complete these mundane steps, listen to your inner guidance for the next step and the next. The key is to follow each step and know you are progressing on your spiritual path. Continue to ignore negative self-talk and just keep going.

Honor your resistances when you have difficulty putting into practice what you know is right for you. Listen to your intuition and see that you may need to finish some loose ends in your life; work on a relationship, raise your children, or do more inner-healing work, such as changing your negative self-talk. When stuck, ask for help. Something will eventually catch your attention, such as an idea or "message" from a TV talk show or a friend calling to tell you about a special book s/he just read.

It is a valuable purpose to do your job well, raise a child, or to provide financial support for your family. Your spiritual purpose may be to heal yourself in order to be your true, authentic self in all your daily experiences. Some of you will receive a deeper calling to impact others outside yourself and family. Those of you responding to a deeper call may receive one step at a time, whereas others may be given a theme, such as writing, or a new career choice, or even a glimpse of the big picture. Now begin answering the questions on the Life Purpose Inventory for deeper awareness of self.

LIFE-PURPOSE INVENTORY

1. List your talents, interests, and gifts (you may or may not be using them). Write about one that you would like to nurture.
2. What are things you love to do when you have the time? What do you enjoy?
3. What are things you see others doing or wish you could do if time, education, and money were not an issue? What might be the "perfect" job or career for you?
4. Write about a significant religious or spiritual experience you have had and how it impacts your life.
5. What do you think or feel would make your family, community, or the world a better place? What small part might you play to bring this about?
6. Discuss the major emotional events, traumas, or challenges that have influenced or shaped your life? Write about how they might motivate you to get involved in making changes in the world, in people's awareness, or to help others with similar issues or problems.
7. Write the most exciting future you can think of for yourself.
8. Who do you respect, admire, and wish to emulate? Explain. Write about possibilities where you might do some of the same things that you admire?
9. List the lessons you feel you have learned so far in life. Write about the ones that are still in process. (Clue: Lessons are brought to awareness where you experience conflict or dissatisfaction.)
10. What might you have to teach others who are a step behind you working through similar issues or challenges as yourself?
11. What do others say when they compliment you? Use your imagination and explore how these traits could be used in a greater way.
12. What childhood memories are themes in the patterns that you repeat in your adult life? Explain how some of these may be motivators to help you heal yourself and then model your process to others.
13. Pray or meditate asking God, a spiritual teacher, guide, angel, or wise person to give you insights about your spiritual purpose. See, hear, or feel answers which can come to you in insights, dreams, daydreams, etc. Write them down and discuss.
14. Write about joy and fulfillment.
15. Do you think your purpose is more about doing or being? Write freely what comes to mind.
16. Sit quietly and allow anything else that your unconscious wants to express to flow onto your paper.

Suzanne E. Harrill, M.Ed., Counselor, Teacher, Author: www.InnerworksPublishing.com

Guided Meditation

Directions: You may read this into a tape recorder to play back to yourself or have someone read it to you. Speak slowly. Soft music may be played in the background.

"Close your eyes and take some deep breaths... As you inhale, breathe in love and peace and calmness... As you exhale, let go of tension, fear, and any tightness in your body... Go to your place of peace... Use your imagination to create this place or remember one you've been to... If you are not a visual person, feel your place of peace... See and feel golden, white light shining on the top of your head, filling you up with healing energy... Imagine the excess flowing from your hands and feet... Feel deep peace and calm.

Imagine a wise teacher or your future wise self joining you in your place of peace... Feel unconditional love radiating towards you... Deep breathe and let it in... Take a few moments to formulate a question that you would like insight into; such as, what is the next step on your journey or how do you heal your relationship with someone in your life or what is your spiritual purpose... Listen and allow insights to flow into your awareness... You may simply ask for deep peace and courage to move forward. (Silence for a few minutes).

Now feel your future self speaking the following affirmations to you. Picture and feel as if they are already true for you. (Read the affirmations on page 66).

It is now time to come back to this room... You can return to your place of peace at any time that you sit quietly and deep breathe... Feel as if you have had a restful nap... Become aware of your body... When you are ready, slowly open your eyes and begin moving and stretching. You are alert and able to drive home safely to continue your day."

Suzanne E. Harrill, M.Ed., Counselor, Teacher, Author: www.InnerworksPublishing.com

Affirmations for Inner Healing

1. I am at peace with myself and accept my oneness with all life.

2. I draw from the wellspring of the Source to fill my heart with love, joy, peace, beauty, and grace. As I fill myself I have more than enough to nourish myself and others.

3. My wisdom guides me moment by moment to know how to act, how to think, and what to say.

4. I accept the rhythm of life with its periods of great activity and fellowship with others and its slow periods giving me the opportunity to assimilate what I have learned and tune into myself.

5. I feel safe and secure, knowing the greater wisdom of the Universe (Spirit, God, Higher Power) is always there to listen, comfort, guide, teach, and heal me through meditation and prayer.

6. As I learn to connect more and more with my true Self, I give up all pain and suffering that I have caused myself by my misperceptions, beliefs, attitudes, actions, and choices. I fully accept responsibility for my life and find deeper meaning behind all experiences.

7. I forgive myself for being unaware and for allowing situations to continue that did not support my highest good and spiritual intentions.

8. I forgive others in order to stop the wounds of the past from coloring the present. I accept the power of Love to heal all pain and suffering so I can extend love to all others, even those whom I choose not to have an active relationship with, those that I dislike, or those who have hurt me. Current grievances roll off my back like water off a duck.

9. In my new world nothing is a mistake, everything is of value for the upliftment of my consciousness. I take full responsibility to be the gardener of my life, continually planting new seeds of transformation and pulling the weeds of my miscreations.

10. Today is a new beginning in consciousness and I use my creative power to draw to me situations and people that help me heal emotionally and spiritually, to move forward, and to actualize my potential.

11. I rejoice in my new life as I live from the full place of Unconditional Love, Light, and Power. I play the hand I was dealt willingly, joyfully, creatively, and with awareness. I love myself and appreciate my life.

Read these affirmations when you go to sleep and when you awaken. Record them.

Suzanne E. Harrill, M.Ed., Counselor, Teacher, Author: InnerworksPublishing.com

Appendix I

Self-Esteem Awareness
Can Improve Your Effectiveness as a Group Facilitator

How can you, a group facilitator, benefit from understanding ways self-esteem affects the group process? You have a very important job, facilitating other people's growth and healing. As a group facilitator you provide the tone of the group, which is influenced by your personality, experiences, awareness, and wisdom. Each group you facilitate will be different from each previous group and that is good and as it needs to be. This way the people attracted to your group will receive exactly what you have to offer. At the foundation of your facilitating is your own self-esteem. Know with humility that you are healing yourself as you help people a step behind you on the path of life. Let us look at self-esteem to help prepare you for your service to other's awareness process.

Simply defined, self-esteem is how you feel about yourself. It is based upon what you tell yourself with self-talk, beliefs you have about yourself, and the self-images you see in your mind. These can be true, partially true, or even false and destructive. A person perpetuates their level of self-esteem without even knowing s/he is sending her/himself so many messages. Let us look a little deeper at self-esteem and how it might be helpful for a facilitator to have an indication of self-esteem levels and issues in a group.

People with low self-esteem have several things in common. Usually they feel little control over their own lives and continually feel victimized by situations and others. They base their sense of worth externally, many times on other people's opinions and belief systems without being able to objectively evaluate them. There is a point over which one crosses where high self-esteem begins. Here a person begins to have more of an internal locus of control, feeling less of a victim, understanding that s/he has something to do with what happens to her/him, or at least understands that s/he has some control over the part played in each situation. As the self-esteem grows, a person learns to set appropriate boundaries with others. Eventually, there is the ability to foresee consequences as life dramas and patterns repeat themselves, thus being able to say, "No," to some experiences or to change them. One begins living consciously as a creative, self-expressive, self-actualizing individual.

A person with high self-esteem feels empowered from within and makes choices with awareness, taking responsibility for paying the consequences, both good and bad, of these choices. The self-talk is no longer overly critical, but supportive and encouraging. The belief system is in a continual process of being updated to correct dysfunctional patterns of thinking to include higher truths. This person sees her/himself in a more realistic light, sending positive images to self, as well. A person with sound self-esteem takes quiet comfort in knowing and accepting her/himself. Growing spiritually is important, too, and the journey to discover one's essence or true Self is important.

A basic rule-of-thumb to identify low self-esteem in others is to look for extremes in thoughts, feelings, and behaviors. We sometimes get tricked into thinking low self-

esteem is only at the end of the continuum with the people-pleasers, those who talk softly, hold back, and cannot easily express thoughts and opinions, and those who do not feel powerful enough to take action to solve their own problems. These people do have issues with low self-esteem, as do those on the opposite side of the low self-esteem coin. People who are self-centered, unaware of their affect on others, aggressive, and who control and dominate others with their opinions and actions, also suffer from low self-esteem.

The pathway to high self-esteem requires taking positive risks to grow in the ability to live life from an internal place of power. Awareness is the key to growing into sound self-esteem.

A facilitator will do a better job running her/his group by looking at and understanding her/his own self-esteem, including areas of vulnerability. The degree to which you value yourself sets the tone of the group as you model and mirror your self-esteem to others. As you grow in loving yourself, you automatically have a positive impact on others' self-esteem, their willingness to participate in the group, and their willingness to take positive risks to heal. It is important to know most people need a boost in some areas of their self-esteem and that there are no perfect facilitators. You are healing yourself as you help others heal.

It is helpful to adjust your teaching style and level of expectation by observing the functioning level of the group participants. Some need more explanations and reassurance, some do not like to share, and some like to share too much. An example of a problem that could arise if a facilitator does not keep her/his own areas of low self-esteem in check might be, to take it personally when one of the following occurs: a participant is quiet and does not wish to participate in the group, does not put into practice anything that would help her/him grow, disagrees or challenges the facilitator, or leaves the group early. The lower the self-esteem level of the facilitator, the more invested s/he is in outside feedback that s/he is doing a good job, so a resistant participant will trigger feelings of failure or not doing a good job. On the other hand, the facilitator must be aware to not become enamored by too much praise and feel like a good facilitator simply because s/he is liked. In other words, it is important to know you are not responsible for someone else's experience or progress. You simply provide information and the space for others to experience what you have to offer with your personal style of facilitating.

It is important to build awareness of your own self-esteem, as well as each participant's. As a group facilitator, you help others heal core issues, self-esteem being a major issue for many people. As you remember, with humility, that you are growing in awareness yourself, then you will do a great job helping others. Enjoy the privilege of facilitating other's healing, growth, and awareness. I wish you well on your journey!

Appendix II
Relationship Enrichment Cards

Couples interested in opening communication and building intimacy with a partner may copy the following and cut them into cards. They may also be used for journal writing and then dialoging with a partner. These cards also build awareness, understanding, trust, and closeness.

Directions: One person draws a card and answers the question, while the partner simply listens. Then the partner answers the same question. When each person is finished answering, each may respond to what the other has said. It may be enough to answer only one question at one sitting.

Or the partners may journal write about the question and then talk. Again, one person at a time speaks while the other listens. When both have taken a turn, each may respond to what has been said.

Copy on cardstock and cut:

Give some one-word descriptions of your relationship at this time.	Rate the degree of compatibility you feel with your partner's personality on a scale of 1-10. Has this changed over time? Explain. How do you feel about this?
Acknowledge your partner for several things s/he has contributed to the relationship.	How would you evaluate your degree of satisfaction with your relationship at this time? Has this changed over time? Explain. How do you feel about this?
Acknowledge yourself for several things you have contributed to the relationship.	It would improve our communication if I _____.

What are the traits that you admire most in your partner?

It would improve our relationship if I _____.

What are the traits that you admire most in yourself?

Describe some polarities (opposites) you and your partner experience in regard to your personalities and habits. Express how you feel about this.

What single trait of your partner is challenging for you? Explain what this brings up for you? What does it tell you about yourself?

Describe some polarities (opposites) you and your partner experience in regard to goals. Express how this affects you.

What single trait of yourself is the most challenging for your partner? Express how this affects you.

Describe some polarities (opposites) you and your partner experience with regard to lifestyle. Express how you feel about this?

Where do you think your relationship needs improvement today?

Describe some polarities (opposites) you and your partner experience with regard to your upbringings. How does this affect you?

Ask your partner for one thing that you need at this time from her/him. Look your partner in the eyes.

What habit bothers you the most about your partner? Explain how it makes you feel, react, behave, etc.

What is one thing you feel or think your partner needs from you today? How do you know?	What habit bothers your partner the most about you? How does it make you feel?
Describe your physical relationship with your partner at this time. Are you content with this? Explain.	List interests you and your partner have in common with each other. Are you satisfied with this? Explain.
Talk about your day-to-day compatibility with your partner.	Are you and your partner compatible with sleep and rest cycles? Express any feelings you have that bother you about this.
Describe your emotional relationship with your partner at this time. Are you okay with this? Explain.	Discuss the need each of you has for affection. How do you feel about this?
Describe your social needs with others and your partner. Are you satisfied with the way things are? Explain.	How do you resolve differences in your relationship?
Describe your mental compatibility with your partner. Are you satisfied with this? Explain.	How do children (your children, stepchildren, desire for children) affect this relationship?

Talk about anger in this relationship. How do you handle your anger? How does your partner? What would you like to say?	Discuss the need each of you has for physical contact. Do you match up on this? Express your feelings.
Describe your spiritual relationship with your partner at this time.	Talk about your spiritual compatibility with your partner at this time.
Express some of your social needs.	Give some one-word descriptions of yourself and of your partner.
Express some of your physical needs.	Give some one-word descriptions of your relationship before marriage. Your your relationship as it is now.
Express some of your emotional needs.	What attracted you to your partner in the beginning of your relationship?
Express some of your mental needs.	How do you manage your feelings of disappointment? Share your process.

Express some of your spiritual needs.	When did you feel a deep sense of commitment towards your partner and the relationship? Has it changed over time? Talk about your process.
What do you need from your partner to improve your relationship?	Are you satisfied with the level of trust and commitment in your relationship? Explain.
What did you learn from your mother about money? Your father? How has this impacted your relationship?	What did you learn from you mother about leisure time? Your father? How has this impacted your relationship?
What do you feel would improve this relationship regarding issues about money?	What do you feel would improve this relationship regarding issues about leisure time?
What did you learn from your mother about time? Your father? How has this impacted your relationship?	What do you feel would improve this relationship regarding time issues?
What did you learn from your mother about sex? Your father? How has this influenced your relationship?	What do you think would improve your sexual relationship?

What did you learn from your mother about love and affection? Your father? How has this affected your relationship?

What do you think would improve your relationship over issues about love and affection?

Rank order from easiest to most difficult these four issues: time money, sex, children.

How do you resolve differences over childrearing?

Self-Help Books by Suzanne E. Harrill

Adults

Seed Thoughts for Loving Yourself: Cultivating the Garden of Your Mind

*Enlightening Cinderella Beyond the Prince Charming Fantasy

A Simple Self-Esteem Guide (Booklet)

*Empowering You to Love Yourself (e-book only)

*Inner Fitness for Creating a Better You: Six Lessons for Building Greater Awareness, High Self-Esteem, Good Relationships, and Spiritual Meaning

* E-books at www.InnerworksPublishing.com

Forthcoming Book

Becoming the Person You Always Wanted to Marry:
  Relationship as a Path to Wholeness

Adolescents

Empowering Teens to Build Self-Esteem

Exploring * Connecting * Emerging
   6wk. Adolescent Self-Esteem Curriculum w/worksheets

For Children

I Am a STAR, My Building High Self-Esteem Book

I Am a STAR: Self-Esteem Affirmation Cards

Order on-line with credit card www.InnerworksPublishing.com

Sign up for free on-line newsletter to spark the inner journey!

www.InnerworksPublishing.com

Suzanne E. Harrill

Suzanne inspires people to build awareness and improve their lives through counseling, coaching, writing, workshops, and public speaking. She is a natural teacher, encourages self-discovery, and facilitates others in becoming their own authority. Empowering clients to heal their own life, to build a solid foundation of self-esteem, and to live with meaning and purpose are top priorities in her work. In the state of Texas Suzanne is a Licensed Marriage and Family Therapist and a Licensed Professional Counselor.

Moving many times with her husband and family to other parts of the US, and twice to Australia, provided many rich experiences with people, cultures, and ideas. Each place received her warmly as she continued her counseling, teaching, and public speaking.

Originally trained as an art teacher, Suzanne later earned her masters degree in education, specializing in counseling psychology. Her experience includes teaching children, adolescents, and college students. In 1981 she started her private counseling practice and began teaching self-esteem workshops for adults. Her first book, published in 1987, initiated her writing career. See her many works on her website.

The mission statement of Innerworks is, "To empower people to love and accept themselves, to heal pain from the past, to know their purpose, and to reach their potential individually and collectively." *Inner Fitness for Creating a Better You* does just that. It is the product of the wisdom gathered over her lifetime and is a great contribution to help others on the journey of self-discovery and inner healing.

Suzanne is married, has three grown daughters, is a grandmother, has a dog, and currently lives in Houston, Texas. She enjoys traveling, hiking in nature, watercolor painting, creating original stained glass pieces, and spending time with her family and friends.

Contact website for free on-line newsletter, to order books, or personal telephone consultations/coaching.
Innerworks Counseling & Publishing   Phone: 303-257-7994

www.InnerworksPublishing.com

Cultivating The Garden of Your Mind  Suzanne E. Harrill

New!

Daily affirmations for cutivating the garden of your mind. Psychological and spiritual truths to help guide you on your inner journey, whether new to self-discovery or a seasoned traveler.
4 x 6 inches
ISBN
9-781-883648-16-9
$14.95

Suzanne E. Harrill
M.Ed.,LPC,LMFT
Licensed Counselor: Individuals, Couples, Families, and Groups
Teacher: Trainer, Professional Speaker, Classes and Workshops
Life Coach: Self Esteem, Spiritual Meaning, Relationships

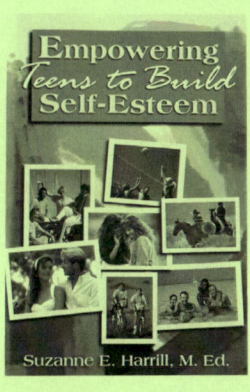

Quick read for busy teens. Esteem Inventory. Peer Pressure questions. Codependence & Dating tips.
ISBN 978-1-883648-04-6 $16.95

10 years later, Fairy Godmother returns to teach how to live happily ever after with or without the prince. An enchanting story full of self-help tips for inner healing and improving relationships.
ISBN 1-899171-58-4 $12.95

Easy-to-Understand lessons to create a new life. Self-study or use to facilitate a group. Handouts/exercises, relationship enrichment cards.
ISBN 1-883648-11-4 $24.95

16 pages full of helpful ideas to build self-esteem.
ISBN 1-883648-09-2
$3.00

Early readers love this little affirmation book on rainbow-colored pages with star graphics. Simple affirmations to build positive self-talk.
ISBN 978-0-9625996-3-7 $12.95

Affirmation cards with star graphics. Comments on back generate discussion.For children, teens, adults reparenting their inner child.Star eraser.
ISBN 1-883648-08-4 $14.95

INNERWORKS
PUBLISHING